THE Billboard BOOK OF
RHYTHM

THE Billboard BOOK OF
RHYTHM

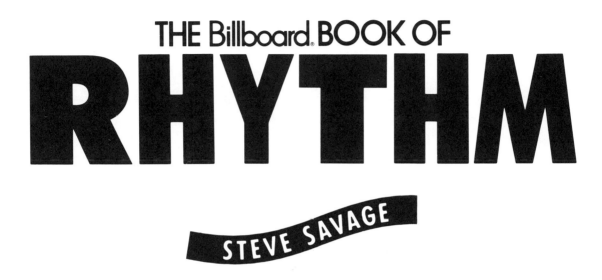

STEVE SAVAGE

BILLBOARD BOOKS
An imprint of Watson-Guptill Publications/New York

Photo Credits on Page 204

First published 1989 by Billboard Books, an imprint of
Watson-Guptill Publications, a division of Billboard
Publications, Inc., 1515 Broadway, New York, NY 10036

Library of Congress Cataloging-in-Publication Data
Savage, Steve
    The Billboard book of rhythm / by Steve Savage.
        p. cm.
    Bibliography: p.
    Includes index.
    ISBN 0-8230-7538-9
    1. Musical meter and rhythm—Instruction and study.   2. Popular
music—Instruction and study.   3. Percussion instruments—Studies
and exercises.   4. Electronic percussion instruments—Instruction
and study.   I. Title
MT42.S3 1989
781.6'2—dc19   88-38664
                                                            CIP
                                                            MN

Manufactured in the United States of America
First printing, 1989
1 2 3 4 5 6 7 8 9 / 94 93 92 91 90 89

"This is dedicated to the one I love": Darlene Jody

ACKNOWLEDGMENTS

THANKS TO TAD LATHROP, who has truly been as much collaborator as editor, and to my brother Marc for support both technical and moral. Thanks also to William F. Ludwig Jr. for the history of the drum set, to Blue Bear School of Music for seventeen great years, and to Lynn Chu for the initial impetus. For musical support while writing this book, thanks to The Sneetches and Bongo People.

CONTENTS

FOREWORD

A LOOK INTO THE PAST reveals a musical history marked by innovation, discovery, and ever-changing approaches to composition, performance, and even music appreciation. Evolving technology has played a particularly powerful role in this development. The refinement of the modern orchestra, for example, enabled composers to expand the range of their compositions. The building of new instruments, and the improvement of old ones, afforded musicians greater flexibility in their performance of music. The advent of modern recording and the acceptance and spread of long-playing disks and tape gave audiences the ability to *own* performances of their favorite music and play it in their homes, at times of their choosing.

The rhythmic aspect of music has been similarly affected by technical and artistic innovations over the years. With the introduction of new instruments and the blending of ideas from around the world, the production of rhythm has expanded to include an endless, internationally-based array of tone qualities and rules for building patterns of drum beats.

Today we are witnessing what is perhaps the richest, most concentrated period of technical innovation in musical history—a modern Age of Digital Technology. New ways of playing, writing, recording, and printing music are cropping up faster than the time it takes to master yesterday's new electronic device. The novice (and not-so-novice) musician is faced with a staggering array of instruments that include drum machines, keyboard and guitar synthesizers, sequencers, samplers, personal computers and music software, and the MIDI digital interface. What this has done is place *all* the tools of music production—including the sounds of drum sets and multi-percussion—literally at the fingertips of people who might otherwise be specializing in one narrow aspect of music. Today songwriters, arrangers, jingle writers, instrumentalists, recording engineers, owners of home recording setups, and just about anyone else with a spark of musical energy, all have direct access to the entire spectrum of musical sound—without having to use auxiliary musicians.

With the proper equipment a songwriter can punch in a measure of rhythm on a drum machine, copy and edit it to the length of a song, record it on a computer sequencer in sync with his own keyboard parts that can sound like anything from marimbas to trumpets, and then, with the push of a few buttons, transfer the entire arrangement to a four-track home cassette recorder. Within minutes, a near-master-quality recording has been created. These are capabilities beyond the wildest dreams of musicians working just a few decades ago.

The new technology makes brand new demands on the musician's base of knowledge. Along with an adventurous willingness to tackle the mechanics of digital technology must come a firm grasp of the basic musical language that is still at the core of the new tech world. The traditions of music and rhythm continue to provide a solid foundation for even the most space-age musical excursions. *The Billboard Book of Rhythm* aims to link the new with the old, to provide a bridge between the world of the known—the nature, form, history, technique, and role of rhythm in music—with the new: the computer-driven sound devices that are putting new means of producing rhythm into the hands of drummers and non-drummers alike. Traditional means of creating rhythm need to be understood before the new techniques made possible by computer programming can be used most effectively.

The Billboard Book of Rhythm is directed toward the contemporary musician who is ready to embark on a journey into the world of drum beats and percussion, whether focusing on traditional instruments or on drum machines. It is intended as a manual in the sense that it provides the music creator with guidelines for setting up rhythms appropriate to the standard styles of today's pop music, and tells how to perform and record them using the new technology. But more than that, it seeks to show the traditions and practices from which current rhythms evolved, to provide a broader context for a musician's current rhythmic activity. A player who knows how drum beats have come to sound the way they do will have a strong basis for deciding where and when to use particular rhythms and how to create usable new patterns of his own.

Part One, "Rhythm Basics," explores the fundamentals of rhythm and pulse in the natural world, and outlines the rudiments of the notational system that has served as the universal means by which musical and rhythmic ideas are written down and communicated. It offers a series of practice rhythms to encourage "thinking like a drummer," and briefly describes the traditional percussion instruments that have served as the models for current drum machine sound libraries.

Part Two, "The Roots of Modern Rhythm," looks at the evolution of rhythm in Western music. Although this is somewhat removed from the pop and rock focus of most readers, it provides a helpful context for the later discussion of African rhythmic influences on all strata of contemporary pop styles. The final part of this section lays out some broad approaches to modern rhythm drawn from the traditions of rock, jazz, and non-Western cultures, and paves the way for a more detailed rundown of popular drum beats.

Part Three, "Drum Beats in Popular Music," provides a listing of rhythms used in pop styles like rock, funk, jazz, country, reggae, and Latin music. These may be used as the basis for setting up drum tracks on home recording equipment, building a vocabulary of rhythm ideas, or simply appreciating the drum tracks on commercial recordings. These sample beats can be very helpful in allowing a non-drummer to "get inside" the standard patterns and techniques that drummers employ at the drum set. In each style presented, the beats are developed from basic patterns to more complex rhythms. By following this logic it is possible to see how different stylistic approaches are interrelated and quite similar.

Part Four, "Drum Machines and the New Technology," provides basic information on drum machine programming and auxiliary functions, and addresses the tricky issue of "feel"—how to avoid a robot-like sound (the bane of most electronic music) and make the machines sound human. This section also details the general functions of MIDI, sequencers, samplers, personal computers, and electronic drums, and offers tips on recording drums and percussion.

As with all great periods of innovation and development, the current revolution has triggered a debate over the ultimate value of the new technology, and whether it will have some sort of negative impact on human musical creativity. The current general perception, following a period of adjustment and acceptance, is that drum machines and other computer-based musical instruments are simply serving as useful new tools, and will never replace the musician or the creative element in music. At their best, they are providing a bridge between the old and the new, between the traditional approaches to music and an infinitely variable library of sounds and sound combinations. As intriguing and futuristic as computer-based instruments may be, they'll never eclipse the need for good, old-fashioned music-making. If anything, they make the process more exciting.

Throughout the computer explosion, with its impact on the forms of musical presentation, on tonal content, and on the process of creation, the essential creative impetus and need for musical expression have remained intact. A basic desire to make music is what ultimately fuels all the technology. The *Book of Rhythm* is offered with this as the underlying message, and it is hoped that readers will find it useful as they attempt to turn their own creative ideas into musical reality.

TAD LATHROP, *Editor*

PART ONE

RHYTHM
BASICS

1
RHYTHM, PULSE, AND NATURE

RHYTHM IS ALL AROUND US. It is a part of our essential nature and is basic to the world we live in. It permeates the natural environment, marks off the passage of time, and is present in the movement of things, man-made and otherwise. Rhythm runs deep.

But it is in popular music that rhythm is most obviously and undeniably present. There it provides a true driving force. At the core of every pop song is an underlying beat or groove that instantly defines the feel of the music and tells the listener how to respond, whether to move in time with an uptempo dance rhythm, or to slow down in preparation for a smooth, flowing ballad. The beat of the music, if played with precision and skill, is what first reaches out and impels us to keep on listening.

The human affinity for rhythm is undeniable. Whatever the beat, whatever the musical style, it's the rhythmic thrust that ultimately drives the song home. Think of the sound of a high-tech commercial dance tune, rolling out of twin speakers on a wave of funky hits, rimshots and backbeats of programmed synthesizer rhythm. Or the sound of jazz, radiating swing-based triplets, finger snaps, kick drum accents, and walking bass lines. Or crunchy rock and roll, with its powerful backbeat and propulsive forward motion. They all tie into an unspoken human feeling, matching the tempo and thrust of our own internal rhythms.

Take a look at the underlying rhythms of hit songs and you'll find much of what put the "popular" in pop music. When the Beatles first arrived on the scene (with a name that matched the momentum of their music) they were hailed for bringing a "big beat" approach to the otherwise tame sound of hit radio. Their knack for locking into a catchy backbeat rhythm went a long way toward fueling the fires of mid-sixties Beatlemania. And Elvis Presley, only a few years before, worked similar magic with his own brand of gyrating rock and roll (a term not without rhythmic reference), basing his chart-topping sound on a loose blend of country music and hip-shaking rhythm and blues. Without a doubt, the broad appeal of popular music has been due in good part to its outgoing sense of rhythm, connecting with this fundamental facet of human nature.

Becoming a Rhythmist. What this means for the rhythm-making musician of today is that a solid sense of rhythm—and how it works in various styles of music—is absolutely essential for getting a message across to audiences. Whatever your musical background, whether it be as a drummer, a guitarist, a songwriter, an arranger, or a user of home recording equipment, chances are your ultimate goal is to write, or play, or record the best music possible, with rhythms that really complement your musical vision. To do this you're going to have to learn more—much more—about all aspects of your craft, building up a firm foundation of knowledge and skill to develop effective rhythms and to function smoothly in the creative, professional world of music.

If you're a drummer, you probably have a particular brand of music that you think of as your specialty. You may have delved deeply into jazz, following in the footsteps of Elvin Jones, Buddy Rich, or Max Roach. Or you might have focused on hard rock and heavy metal, developing a shotgun snare sound and a double-barreled kick drum technique. But there's much more out there. Keep in mind that branching out and picking up ideas from all areas of music is only going to add to your rhythm arsenal, giving you the tools to work in a number of contexts, and providing new fuel for the development of your own favorite drum style. It's also important to get on top of the new technology that's beginning to dominate the music scene, especially the drum machines that you've probably feared will put you out of work but that are most often being used to *supplement* real drum sounds and performances.

If you're a guitarist or a non-drumming instrumentalist, you may have wandered into the world of drum machines as a way to enrich your home practicing, or to add a professional sound to your demo tapes. Naturally, you're going to have to look into the techniques and beats that drummers actually use in the style of music you're playing or recording. More generally, you'll need to begin thinking like a drummer. Learning about accents and time shifting, for example, will help you avoid the mechanical drum sound that makes most demo tapes sound stiff and overly precise.

If you're a songwriter, and are like many other songwriters, you like to vary your repertoire and work in different grooves from song to song. Without a broad background of rhythmic knowledge, you might miss out on some exciting approaches that could inspire a top 10 hit, or at least point you in a new direction. If you happen to be stuck in a particular genre, like straight-ahead rock and roll, trying out ideas from other rhythmic formats will usually break the stalemate and get some fresh creative juices flowing.

If you're a home recording enthusiast, you've probably assembled (or are beginning to assemble) a collection of impressive toys like a DX-7 synthesizer, a four-track cassette deck, a personal computer, and a drum machine. When you recover from the spending binge, you'll find that all the technology in the world won't guarantee a demo tape that contains thoughtful, inspired, or even coherent music. The current myth is that anyone with a little cash can purchase state-of-the-art sequencers, synths, and tape decks and then go on to compete in the real world of professional music composer/producers. The not-so-secret truth is that *not one* money-making producer today is doing it on equipment alone. If you own a drum machine and plan on using it to nail down some effective music tracks, you may as well do it right and learn as much as possible about the drum beats, the stylistic influences, the array of percussion sounds, and the full range of electronic gear that will ultimately be at your disposal.

Rhythm has had a profound influence on the direction and accessibility of contemporary music. To gain a fuller sense of that importance, and to begin plugging into the mechanisms that make rhythm tick, it's worth starting with the basics and looking at the depth of rhythm's roots in nature itself. It is there that the essence of rhythm ebbs and flows, awaiting the force of logic to lend it shape and structure. How *does* rhythm connect with the natural world and with our own physical processes? And how does that reflect back and have an impact on the effectiveness of rhythms we play?

Defining Rhythm. We experience rhythm on a subconscious, purely physical level in the beating of our heart and in the filling of our lungs. We express rhythm in our walk, our talk, and our everyday actions. We hear rhythm in the falling rain, the rustling wind, and the rushing of water. We follow rhythm in poetry, plays, movies, and novels. We see rhythm in painting, sculpture, architecture, and everyday objects. We use rhythm as the essential underpinning of music, especially of the pop music that most of us have grown up with. But how does it all work? And what *is* rhythm, anyway?

The word rhythm is derived from the Greek *rhythmos* which means "measured motion," or put more broadly, "to flow." Rhythm flows as a river flows—not always at the same rate of speed or in the same direction, but always with motion. The flow of our lives might easily be expressed in terms of rhythm.

Broadly speaking, rhythm is tied into our general concept of time. We can't directly see, touch, smell, taste, or hear time. Yet all of our sensations are experienced within its context. Referring back to the Greek concept of *rhythmos* or "measured motion" we find that the "motion" being measured by rhythm is that of time itself.

One way we measure time is in terms of planetary movement using the basic building blocks of seconds, minutes, hours, days, weeks, months, years, decades, and centuries. While there is a definite rhythm in the flow of these large subdivisions of time, the notion of rhythm—the rhythm that we can readily feel and manipulate—is expressed in much smaller units or building blocks.

Both time and rhythm share an element of movement, of forward motion. The mind is constantly attempting to place order on the passage or movement of time, and it does so in a number of common, everyday ways: we "set the pace" of our walk down the street; we schedule our activities to get them done in time. Almost any human activity can be said to have a rhythm that helps us sense temporal movement.

But rhythm can go beyond the simple ordering or measuring of time. By manipulating units of rhythm we can play upon a listener's subtle sense mechanisms and begin to elicit some of the wider gradations of human feeling. When we use rhythm this way, we usually do it in the context of music.

Rhythm in Music. Music itself is a composition in time. Rhythm is essential to music—it is its basic temporal element. Rhythm is the pattern of music in time, the "measured motion" of time in music. It is also an aspect of music that helps us transcend our normal experience of time. In a musical context rhythm may be both the measurement of the movement and the basis of its magic.

The most basic elements of musical experience—such as feelings of excitement or of being soothed—grow out of varied approaches to rhythm. The linkage of rhythm to feeling is suggested in the term "organic rhythm," drawn from the vocabulary of poetry, which describes a rhythmic flow of words designed to match the feeling to be conveyed. In music, tempos and rhythms express feelings in the simple ways that they mimic human experience. A normal musical tempo may be sixty or eighty beats per minute, the average heartbeat is seventy-two bpm, and the natural walking pace seventy-six to eighty steps per minute. Obviously, the pace of a person running will create many more steps per minute and a considerably faster heartbeat. Similarly, certain kinds of music and musical passages employ somewhat faster or slower tempos. Faster tempos—such as those found in current rock styles such as speed metal and funk—often generate an intense degree of excitement. A slow blues will bring out a sense of spaciousness, perhaps suggesting the pain of longing or a feeling of melancholy. Upbeat, irregular phrases—a specialty of new wave bands like Devo—can provoke nervousness or jumpiness. Sometimes a particularly complex rhythm will suggest feelings and responses too difficult to categorize or define. In fact, a single piece of music may elicit different reactions from different people. Yet in all cases rhythm is inextricably tied to human feeling, and to understand this link we need to examine more closely the structure of musical rhythm.

Music generally consists of rhythm, melody, and harmony. Among these elements, rhythm is the most fundamental. Melody and harmony must have a rhythmic context. They require rhythm to place them in time, though they also influence and create rhythm as part of their process of movement. Rhythm, on the other hand, may stand alone as the sole musical element, as in a drum or percussion solo.

Essentially, rhythm consists of all of the elements that pertain to the duration of musical sound. Rhythm in music may be entirely free, using durations of time that aren't derived from a basic unit. (In this sense we may consider nearly any sound as music.) But the most common rhythms are those that rest on a foundation of regularity. Borrowing from the vocabulary of poetry once again, we encounter this definition of rhythm: sounds and silences that fill equal or balancing time periods, recurring with pleasing regularity. Rhythm in music may or may not fit this definition, but most of the time it follows quite strict guidelines.

Rhythm in music is generally formed relative to an underlying pulse (beat) at a given rate (tempo), in regularly numbered (metric) groups. This means that there is a basic unit of time organized into regular and repeating patterns, much as in the rhythm of poetry defined above. Endless patterns may be formed, within a metric context, from notes made up of larger and smaller fractional values of the beat.

The best way to approach some of rhythm's more complex patterns, especially the ones used in pop music, is to first look at one of rhythm's most basic elements and one of its most obvious connections to nature: the pulse.

Rhythm and Pulse. The basic unit into which we divide musical time is called a pulse beat or just a beat. A regular succession of beats creates a pulse. In listening to most music we are instinctively aware of a periodic succession of beats, a pulse, which is underlying the musical rhythm. Sometimes the pulse is hard to hear, and in some forms of music (generally termed free rhythm) it doesn't exist. In most music, however, there is a guiding pulse that is possible for us to follow. The musical pulse is most often the foundation of the musical rhythm, and it comes from some very essential and natural elements of life.

The musical pulse has many counterparts in nature. On the most fundamental level musical pulses tend to correspond to such basic phenomena as the heartbeat and walking, as described earlier. On a higher level, musical pulse can be defined in terms of dance. The proper beat, meaning the rate that we perceive as a beat, is the rate comfortable for dancing (or marching, another aspect of human movement often associated with drums and percussion). Perception of the beat may vary from person to person, but in most instances any person will respond physically to the same level of pulse in a given piece of music. This pulse is called the beat.

Accenting the Pulse. A simple pulse, however, is still lacking one of the other basic elements of rhythm: accent. When presented with an unaccented pulse, people tend to instinctively divide the pulse into groups of two or three, by imagining a stress on the first of every two or three beats. The mind imposes a regular succession of strong and weak beats on an otherwise unaccented pulse. This instinct for stress accenting is closely associated with actions of the body—the natural rhythm of movement in dance on the one hand, and the rhythms of work-oriented movements such as swinging an ax or rocking a cradle on the other. The "pleasing regularity" of the rhythm of poetry is part of this same instinct to group into patterns or measures of time.

Musical rhythm reflects this natural tendency to perceive groups of beats in its use of accentuation, forming a simple pulse with accents. By accenting or stressing notes at regular intervals we create units of time (time-measures), which are fundamental building blocks of rhythm. In the example below, the circles represent pulses. By accenting (darkening) certain pulses we create groupings (or time-measures) of three:

Musicians often express a relationship to the pulse in the way they move their bodies while performing, or, expressed differently, in the way they "groove to the beat." Watch almost any professional musicians in any style of music (or think about your own playing habits), and you will see them keeping a pulse—the beat—with some part of their body. It may be expressed in just a tapping of the foot, or with a large whole-body move-ment, or in a slight nodding of the head—in some way they are translating the beat into a physical movement. And within that motion they are also probably acknowledging the subtle accents that recur in the pulse.

Accenting a pulse is the simplest way rhythm reflects the natural flow of human movement. Without accents, a pulse just becomes a mechanical reminder of the passage of time. One common complaint about today's drum machines is that they all too often sound like glorified mechanical time keepers. When we look at ways to "humanize" drum machines in a later chapter, we'll find that is through varied accenting that we'll best be able to suggest human rhythmic idiosyncrasies.

Pulse Games. The following games may help you begin to feel and internalize the relationship of accents to pulse in the same way that a drummer might. (They will also prepare you for the following chapters on notation and basic rhythms.) By using circles to indicate pulse beats, and darker and lighter shadings to indicate accentuation, you can begin to perform some basic accented pulses.

Each circle represents a pulse beat, and each row of circles is to be clapped around continuously. This means that the final beat in the row should be thought of as falling right before the first beat of the same row, so that the pulse flows continuously from the end of the line back to the beginning. Experiment with different tempos (rates of pulse), but follow two basic guidelines: start slow, and once you've started try to maintain an even pulse (don't slow down or speed up). If you start slow and then wish to try the pulse exercise faster, stop and start again at a faster tempo.

Below is a simple pulse with no accentuation. Clap the pulse at a comfortable tempo. Note that you may naturally tend to group the pulse into twos or threes by creating strong and weak beats. Try to avoid this, and maintain as even a pulse as possible, with no accentuation and no speeding or slowing.

Next, the pulse is grouped into twos by alternating stressed (black) and unstressed (white) circles. Clap at a slow tempo, repeating the pulse around and around several times. Then stop and clap at a quick rate, this time tapping your foot only on the stressed beats. You now have two pulses going—the quicker clapping pulse and the slower tapping pulse. This is the beginning of rhythm within a simple musical context. The faster pulse, with alternating stresses, may be considered a basic musical rhythm while the tapping foot keeps the underlying beat (the slower pulse) at a comfortable physical tempo.

Now the pulse will be grouped into threes through stressed and unstressed pulse beats. Clap and tap this at different tempos—clapping the pulse with accents as shown, tapping your foot on only the stressed beats.

● ○ ○ ● ○ ○ ● ○ ○ ● ○ ○

In the next example the groupings which are created by the stressed beats are no longer regular. Although still a simple pulse, the accentuation is creating groupings of different lengths. This creates more interest and a stronger sense of motion. Try tapping your foot on every other pulse beat as you clap this rhythm. This can be very difficult as one of the stressed beats falls in between foot taps. Try it first without the accents. When you're comfortable, begin to clap the accents. In this exercise the foot is keeping the beat and the clapping is creating rhythm through accenting.

Next are some other pulses with irregular stresses. These may be played as individual rhythms, repeating over and over from the end of each line back to the beginning. You may also try playing through from the top line through each descending line to the last line and then back again to the top. Try clapping the pulse with just the accents first, then try tapping and clapping. First tap on every other pulse beat (in 2) then try every third pulse beat (in 3). Notice how the visual representation of these pulse rhythms reflects the way design is a part of the musical concept. Some of the exercises may be very difficult to coordinate at first.

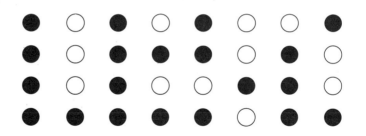

The example below has three levels of stress—black for the primary accent, gray indicating a secondary accent (accented, but not as strongly as for a black circle), and white for unaccented. The cycle created is a four-beat cycle: the first beat accented, the second unaccented, the third with a secondary accent, and the fourth unaccented. Try clapping this pulse rhythm at different tempos. Because the cycle is regular, containing four pulses or beats, this rhythm is again describing a time-measure (or simply a "measure") though a more involved one than the two- and three-beat measures from the earlier examples. This type of four-beat cycle is central to musical rhythm.

Using varied shadings, as in the next examples, it is possible to create complex patterns of accentuation.

This method of visualizing is one way of writing down and communicating rhythmic ideas. It is a simple form of music notation. The more universally used form of rhythmic notation is a more complex and flexible system. Knowledge of it is necessary for the operation of most all drum machines and sequencers, and will help you to create and play some quite complicated beat patterns.

Learning Rhythms. At first glance this section title might not make a lot of sense. Many people feel that rhythmic skill is completely instinctive—something you either have or you don't.

Actually, this couldn't be much further from the truth. In psychological tests, infants have been shown to respond to tonal patterns in a way that is similar to the way they respond to spoken language. To be human is to be capable of making music, just as to be human is to be capable of speech.

As with language, the capacity to learn music changes as a child grows older. Tests show that the affinity for rhythmic development hits a peak when a child reaches the age of about eleven to twelve years old, and then it begins to taper off. It's true that people who receive training at early ages will tend to exhibit higher degrees of musical ability later in life. It's also true that a person with no formal training as a child, raised in a non-music- or movement-oriented environment, may struggle to learn to express rhythm when attempted at a later age. Nonetheless, as studies bear out, to be human is to be capable of music, and though it may be difficult at first to try to connect with some of the instinctive elements of rhythm, it is possible for anyone to attain a high level of rhythmic and musical ability at any age.

New technology and computer programs have provided a fast entry into the world of music for interested non-musicians. This "opening of doors" is revolutionary in its potential for increasing music participation, yet it raises questions about the value and necessity of acquiring a basic knowledge of music. If you can program listenable music by pressing a few buttons, why take the time to bone up on old-fashioned skills that may soon become obsolete? There are several reasons.

Learning to use a drum machine without ever learning various types of rhythm combinations will limit the range of music you'll be able to perform or program on your electronic gear. Chances are you'll end up programming only as much music as you have in your own memory bank. So to increase your rhythm vocabulary it's well worth exploring the drum beats and styles that are currently in use. Knowledge of the physical act of drumming is also helpful. Although you can set up drum machine rhythms without the ability to "keep a beat," having knowledge of musical coordination and the way drummers work and think will greatly enhance your ability to "humanize" the new tech sounds. "Keeping the beat" is a natural part of our musical sense and needs to be developed by anyone participating in the creation of music, whether on acoustic or electronic instruments.

At its best, music can express the full range of human emotional and intellectual capabilities, yet the process of learning music and musicianship can be as repetitive, mundane, and downright boring as any human endeavor. Initially, you're going to have to narrow your sights on the details and the basics of your craft, so that eventually you'll be able to communicate the broader range of emotion possible through music. The ultimate pay-off is definitely worth the effort.

2

WRITTEN RHYTHM: NOTATION AND DESIGN

TODAY, MORE THAN EVER, THERE IS wide-open opportunity for the untrained musician to get involved in pop music through the use of computer programs, keyboard synthesizers, and drum machines. Unfortunately, many people who might derive pleasure from musical expression are put off by the obstacle of learning musical notation.

There are some valid reasons for "fear of notation," stemming largely from the actual limitations of the note-writing system. In the widely-used Suzuki method for teaching music to young children the standard notational system is not used, at least not until students have acquired basic instrumental technique. The rationale is that notation may be an obstacle for beginners, young or old, because they can inevitably play and compose much more complex music than they can read or notate. Notation tends to draw note-readers away from the way music actually sounds because they are concentrating on the way it appears on paper; the brain tends not to tune into the ear if it's concentrating on the page. Notation may also be an obstacle to artistry by distracting from the subtleties of interpretation and expression.

Still, Suzuki appreciated the ultimate necessity of notation in facilitating the pursuit of music. It simply must be part of a balanced plan, and the importance of learning to read music far outweighs its temporary drawbacks. On the plus side, reading music is much easier to learn than playing a musical instrument. Once the system is understood—and it's not much more complicated than taking fractions of an apple or a pie as you did in elementary school—a basic working understanding can follow very quickly. Notation is the universal language of music, and it is a tremendous aid in organizing and retaining musical ideas, communicating with other musicians, and programming sequencers and drum machines.

Interestingly, while physical coordination is not strictly necessary for the use of drum machines, a basic understanding of notation is. Most of today's music software uses notation as a means by which the user gives musical instructions to whatever synthesizers and drum machines he has hooked up to his home music system.

The following discussion deals with the basics of musical notation and simple rhythms. Most of you aren't eleven or twelve years old any more, so absorbing this information might be a little slow going at first. That's okay. Notation is a useful tool, but it's not the most important part of understanding, playing, or composing music.

It is not the intention of this book to train the reader to become fluent in written music. Fluency takes a lot of time to develop and is generally unnecessary in performing most popular music. What you'll find in this section is only as much notation as is necessary to cover the basic drum beats used in today's pop music—the same drum beats you may want to use as the basis for your own drumming or programmed rhythm tracks. Those of you already familiar with written music may want to skim this chapter and the next, trying the rhythms and refreshing your memory of certain concepts such as meter and syncopation. Those who have never learned to read music, or have only a scant understanding of written music, should probably take your time sifting through this material.

Another valuable point of reference in understanding rhythm is that of design. Visualizing rhythms, thinking of them as designs or patterns, is a useful method of understanding and a valuable adjunct to the notational system. The pulse game from the previous chapter is a good example of the way rhythms may be visually represented. The design aspect of rhythm will be pointed out in some of the following discussions.

Bear in mind that this chapter deals only with the rhythmic side of notation and doesn't touch on melody or harmony. For more complete discussions of notation refer to any introductory music text.

Symbols. Despite Plato's observation that rhythm is "an order of movement," the rhythmic order in some musical compositions may be very difficult to follow. Nonetheless, there are fundamental units of rhythmic order identifiable in most pieces of music. These include the basic elements of beat, tempo, measure, meter, and phrase, as well as the broader concepts of structure and style.

The modern system of notation uses a variety of symbols to represent musical events in time—Plato's "order of movement." The basic system is quite simple, using a relatively small number of symbols to represent musical events. Once you have familiarized yourself with the symbols, along with a few basic principles, most commonly used rhythms are easily understood.

Musical symbols, aside from indicating pitch, represent "relative durations of time." These relative durations of time are expressed as fractions, just as you once separated segments of a pie into fractional parts. The whole note is the largest unit of rhythm, with shorter durations of time expressed as fractions of the whole note. These shorter units are called half note, quarter note, eighth note, sixteenth note, and so on. Each of these notes has its own symbol. A half note adds a stem to a whole note, and a quarter note darkens in the head of the half note. An eighth note adds a flag to a quarter note with flags added on as the value of the notes decreases by half.

Notes are written on a musical staff, which consists of five lines and four spaces:

A musical note indicates a musical sound, and for each note there is an equivalent rest indicating a relatively equal amount of silence. The next page shows the symbols used for the notes and the rests.

NOTES AND RESTS

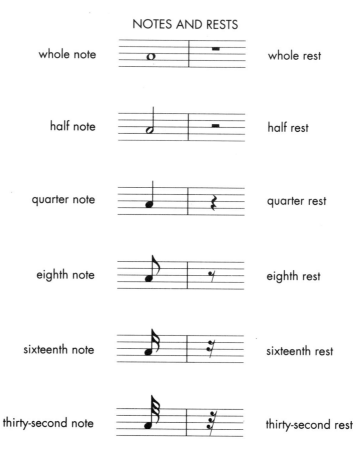

whole note — whole rest

half note — half rest

quarter note — quarter rest

eighth note — eighth rest

sixteenth note — sixteenth rest

thirty-second note — thirty-second rest

Notes with flags on the stems may be grouped together using beams instead of flags. Beams provide a simplified visual approach to the writing of complicated rhythms.

Next are shown the relative values of notes and rests, indicating their basic fractional relationship (one whole note equals two half notes which equals four quarter notes, and so on).

RELATIVE VALUES OF NOTES AND RESTS

These notes and rests are the basis of the entire notational system. Rhythm is primarily the process of dividing up time, and these symbols give us a simple way of representing this. The development of the notational system will correspond to the development of rhythm in music.

Pulse + Tempo = Beat. As we saw in the previous chapter, pulse is the underlying, regular beat present in almost all rhythms. As a basic unit it may be represented by repeated notes of any single given value.

Tempo is the rate of the pulses, meaning the amount of time between each pulse beat. A repeating pulse at a given tempo creates the beat. Conversely, the beat is the combination of a pulse at a tempo. Popular use has blurred the exact meanings of these terms, and you may hear the beat of a song referred to as its pulse, its tempo, or its beat.

The beat remains constant throughout most pieces of popular music. Beat is loosely defined as the rhythmic unit one responds to in dancing or walking. The beat is primarily what ties music to human movement. Tempos are assigned to the beat, and these are shown on paper or on screen with tempo marks or metronome indications. Tempo marks are tempo instructions usually given in their Italian form (e.g., *adagio, allegro*) and are general indications that allow room for interpretation. Metronome tempos are given relative to note values such as $\quarternote$ = 76, indicating that the tempo of the quarter note is seventy-six beats per minute. Drum machines use this metronomic number system for defining the tempo of the rhythm. In live popular music the tempo, or the beat, is usually established by simply "counting in."

Rhythm emerges from patterns of sounds and silences. These patterns are set up relative to a consistent pulse and tempo. The relative value of notes also remains consistent. Thus in the example below the eighth notes will be played twice as rapidly as the preceding quarter notes, no matter what the starting tempo.

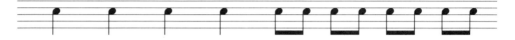

As you can see, the entire notational system is built on relative values. The notes are first relative to the beat and then relative to each other based on their fractional values. In order to make this system work we must assign a note value to the beat. We accomplish this, and also provide a simple way to organize the beats, via the time signature.

Grouping Beats—Time Signatures. It simplifies matters to organize the beats of a piece of music into small groups of equal size, called bars or measures. Measures are separated by bar lines, which are vertical lines through the staff. The number of beats in each measure is constant. (There might be four in each measure, for example.) The time signature, which appears at the beginning of a piece of written music, describes the number of beats in each measure as follows:

top number = number of beats in a measure

bottom number = note value of each beat

The most common time signature is $\frac{4}{4}$ (called "four-four time"), which indicates that there are four beats to the measure (top number) and that each beat is given the value of one quarter note (bottom number). The bottom number is understood to be the bottom of a fraction, thus the bottom 4 in $\frac{4}{4}$ time is read as $\frac{1}{4}$, meaning that a quarter note is being assigned the value of the beat.

In $\frac{3}{4}$ time there will be three beats to the measure, and the beat is again assigned the value of one quarter note.

In $\frac{6}{8}$ time the beat is now assigned the value of one eighth note and there are six of them in each measure.

The bottom number in a time signature must be a multiple of two in order to represent a note value (usually a 4 or 8, meaning a quarter or an eighth note).

Rhythms are created using various values of notes and rests within a time signature. The rhythms work relative to the beat, and must maintain the correct number of beats in each measure. This means that the total value of the notes and rests in any given measure must equal the value and number of beats indicated in the time signature. Thus in any measure of $\frac{4}{4}$ time the notes and rests must add up to four quarter notes' worth of time.

The last measure of the example below contains a $\frac{4}{4}$ time pattern made up of one quarter note, an eighth-note rest, three eighth notes, and then a quarter note. Added together these values equal four quarter notes' worth of time or one measure of $\frac{4}{4}$, as with each of the measures in this example.

The following examples show various simple rhythms in different time signatures. Notice how the values of the notes and rests in each measure add up to the value indicated by the time signature. Notice also that the beams provide a visual aid in identifying individual beats. In general, the physical layout of these rhythms illustrates the nature of design in rhythm notation. Each beat occupies roughly the same physical space (as does each measure), with half notes twice as far from each other as the quarter notes, the quarter notes twice as far as the eighth notes, and so on. Though notation does not require that music be written this way (and it often isn't, given the space limitation of manuscript paper), it does help us visualize the underlying beats of each measure. We will maintain this visual aid in the way rhythms are written throughout this book.

This completes our discussion of the essentials of rhythm notation. Once you are clear on the meaning and relationship of notes, rests, and time signatures, you have grasped the essence of the entire system of written rhythm.

Meter and the Four-Beat Cycle. Time signatures reflect the natural tendency to create music in repetitive cycles of beats. The most common grouping is that of four beats or four-four time, also called the four-beat cycle. It is often called "common time," and, while usually written as $\frac{4}{4}$, is sometimes indicated with a simple C at the beginning of the musical staff. In almost all world cultures the four-beat cycle is the predominant beat cycle. Two- and three-beat cycles are also common, but the four-beat cycle has developed apparently on its own in most musical cultures. Just as music itself is innately human in a way only vaguely understood, the four-beat cycle seems to be an innate preference within the musical language.

Meter, on the other hand, is not nearly as universal as the four-beat cycle. Meter refers to the underlying feeling of accentuation that normally accompanies a time signature. This is a very important rhythmic concept. It is saying that in each beat cycle or measure there are degrees of accent that are felt and subtly translated into our playing of each individual beat. Certain accenting patterns occur naturally, and become standard practice. Like so many other musical rules, these can be followed, bent, played with, or ignored in order to produce a musical effect. World cultures vary widely in the patterns of accents that they apply to the four-beat cycle. In the rhythm of popular music, the meter or underlying accentuation of the four-beat cycle has its own distinctive pattern.

Meter in the Western classical tradition is expressed in terms of accents, secondary accents, and unaccented notes. The classical $\frac{4}{4}$ meter, which differs from the meter you'll find in pop music, is indicated below with a / indicating an accent, a – indicating a secondary accent, and a U indicating an unaccented note.

In this instance it is the 3 beat, the secondary accent, that distinguishes the four-beat cycle from two successive two-beat cycles. If the 3 beat were a primary accent this would be a two-beat meter cycle. The secondary accent creates the four-beat cycle, as you saw in the previous chapter's pulse game where the gray box represented a secondary accent on beat 3.

The following chart shows the standard meter in all of the common time signatures used in the Western classical tradition. Simple meter includes groupings by two, three, and four. Compound meter multiplies each of these by three, giving six, nine, and twelve. You should approach all of your rhythm playing with an awareness of possible underlying feelings of accentuation. Meter represents an important bridge to the subtlety of rhythmic expression.

TIME SIGNATURE			METER			
			simple duple			
2	2	2	/	U		
2	4	8	1	2		
			simple triple			
3	3	3	/	U	U	
2	4	8	1	2	3	
			simple quadruple			
4	4	4	/	U	–	U
2	4	8	1	2	3	4

compound duple

6	6	6	/ U U – U U
2	4	8	1 2 3 4 5 6

compound triple

9	9	9	/ U U – U U – U U
2	4	8	1 2 3 4 5 6 7 8 9

compound quadruple

12	12	12	/ U U – U U – U U – U U
2	4	8	1 2 3 4 5 6 7 8 9 10 11 12

3
PRACTICE RHYTHMS

WITH THE BASICS OF RHYTHM NOTATION under your belt, some simple practice rhythms will help you get better acquainted with the essential building blocks of more extended beat patterns. The best way to approach the following examples is to tap your foot or in some way keep a physical sense of the underlying beat as you clap the rhythm. Begin by tapping your foot with authority until it becomes second nature. Then clap the given rhythms or play them on an instrument. If you have had little or no musical training, this might at first seem a little like rubbing your stomach and tapping your head at the same time, but it is pretty simple once you get the hang of it. Feeling and internalizing the rhythm in this way will help you later on when you begin programming drum machines and wish to avoid stiff or mechanical rhythm patterns.

Eighth-Note Rhythms. Below is a measure of $\frac{4}{4}$ time consisting of an eighth-note pulse. The beat is defined by the time signature as a quarter note, with four quarter notes per measure. In this rhythm we have subdivided each beat into two notes, with two eighth notes equalling one quarter note and eight eighth notes adding up to a complete measure of $\frac{4}{4}$.

An easy way to count this rhythm is to assign a name to each note. The beats (often distinguished more precisely as "primary" beats) are labeled

1, 2, 3, and 4. The intermediary notes, created by our subdivision into eighth notes, are labeled as "and" beats.

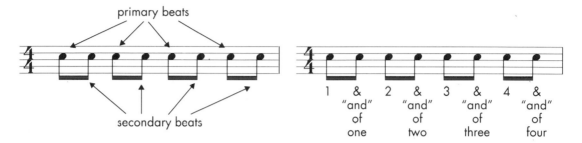

Notice the way the beams (indicating eighth notes) are used. The 1 beat is beamed to the following "and" beat, the 2 beat to the next "and" beat, and so on. This shows the organization of beats. Each beat occupies the time from its beginning up to the beginning of the following beat. Thus the "and" beat following beat 1 is linked with beat 1 (it's connected by a beam, if the rhythm allows), and is correctly termed the "and" of 1. (As we progress through various rhythms be aware of how we use beams to maintain a visual sense of notes that are within the same beat. The use of beams is a great aid in reading rhythms because of the way it allows you to see each independent beat.) Although this example is a simple pulse, it is also a rhythm and you should tap and clap it. Tap on the numbers only; clap on all eight beats. It's helpful to keep track of each note name as you go, counting 1 *and* 2 *and* 3 *and* 4 *and*.

The following examples are in various time signatures, and they use the eighth note as the smallest subdivision. The rhythms should be repeated around and around many times. This means that the pulse or beat should flow directly from the final beat of the final measure back into the first beat of the first measure.

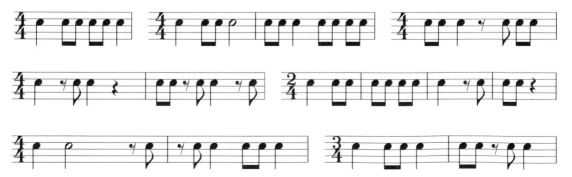

Try creating your own eighth-note rhythms following these examples. You might approach this in two different ways. First, start by imagining the beat alone. Then add a rhythm by filling in certain notes either on the beat or on the eighth note following each beat. Second, you might start off with the eighth-note pulse used at the beginning of this section. Variations may be created by omitting any number of the notes in the pulse. Both ways of thinking about rhythm—as filling an empty space or as making space in a continuous pulse—are valid, and each can suggest different and interesting ideas.

When performing these rhythms remember that it is better to mess up the rhythm and maintain the beat than to lose the beat in trying to stay on top of the rhythm. If you fumble the pattern just let the beat keep coming around to 1 and try again until you can clap the rhythm correctly over the tapping foot.

A metronome can help to reinforce the beat, but don't rely on it to replace the tapping of the foot. *You've* got to keep the beat. It's a good idea to keep mental track of the count as you clap and tap (For example, repeating to yourself 1, 2, 3, 4, 1, 2, 3, 4, in $\frac{4}{4}$). It is also fun to experiment with tempos from slow to fast (sometimes it's harder to play real slow than real fast), and a metronome can help establish the various tempos. Remember that coordination takes repeated practice, but once it's mastered it becomes second nature. Rhythm is in all of us—we must simply help it to the surface.

The Curved Line—Ties and Slurs. The curved line has a variety of uses in music notation, but it serves most often as a tie. A tie joins two notes together to create a longer note. Thus the two tied quarter notes below are equal to one half note.

The tie is useful when a sound is to be sustained over a bar line. For example:

The tie is also used to maintain a visual reminder of the placement of the beat, similar to the way beams are used. The following two rhythms sound identical. One is written with beams and ties, the other with varying note values. While it is important to become familiar with the second kind of notation, the first kind is easier to read: we can *see* where the beats occur.

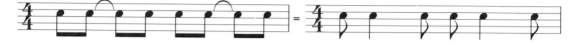

Syncopation. Syncopation is a rhythmic term that is often misused or misunderstood. Broadly defined, syncopation is any abnormality in meter. In practice, this translates into the absence of an accent on a normally accented beat (as defined by the meter) or an accent on a normally unaccented beat. Another definition calls syncopation a lack of coincidence between the rhythm and the beat. Syncopation is so broadly applied in all forms of contemporary music—popular and classical—that the term is only really useful in discussing degrees of syncopation, or the degree to which the rhythm varies from the meter and/or the beat.

A very basic syncopation is shown below. On the left is simple $\frac{4}{4}$ meter, showing primary and secondary accents. On the right, the rhythm leaves out beat 3, defined in classical meter as a secondary accent, and thus creating a syncopation. This also conforms to the idea of a temporary lack of coincidence between the rhythm and the beat—the rhythm here does not play on beat 3, meaning they don't coincide.

In the next example of syncopation, written both with ties and without, we use an eighth-note subdivision to create a more syncopated feeling.

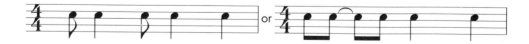

Here the syncopation is created by the absence of beat 2, but the degree of syncopation is greater than in the previous example because of the "and" beats which are played before and after the missing 2 beat. Here we are led from beat 1 to beat 2 by the "and" of 1, but instead of landing on the 2 we skip over it, picking up at the "and" of 2 and finally resolving back to the beat at beat 3. This is a common and important kind of syncopation in all forms of popular music. It can be difficult to master in clapping and tapping but the result will be worth the effort. Part of the advantage of learning rhythm by clapping and tapping is that in a case such as this, the missing 2 beat is "played" by the tapping foot. Try it on the next rhythm, found in the chorus of Carole King's "It's Too Late." This is similar to the previous example except that in the first measure it leaves out both the 2 and the 3 beats, finally resolving on beat 4. Syncopation often excludes more than one of the primary beats in a measure.

In the following two-measure rhythms, you hear this basic type of syncopation applied in various ways. As rhythms become more removed from the beat they also become difficult to read and to coordinate. Some of the rhythms below are written using beams and ties. Others are written using notes of whatever length necessary to create the desired rhythm. Though this style of writing may be initially more difficult to read it has become the more commonly accepted practice.

Notice that in the final two-measure example you play on the 1 beat of measure 1 and then play only the "and" beats through the rest of measure 1 and throughout measure 2. This rhythm suggests what is called a "cross pulse." A cross pulse is one that runs contrary to the beat in some manner. Cross pulses can be extended into polyrhythms, which we'll look at in a later chapter.

The one-measure rhythm below is a very common syncopated rhythm. Notice that the time from beat 1 to the "and" of beat 2 is one and one-half beats, or a quarter note plus an eighth note.

There is another symbol that is used in notation to create this length of note. A note with a dot following the note head—called a dotted note— indicates that the value of the note is extended by one half of the value of the note that is written. Thus a dotted quarter note is equal to a quarter note plus an eighth note, a dotted half note is equal to a half note plus a quarter note, and so on. The dotted note is extremely common in written music. The rhythm above is rewritten here using the dotted quarter note.

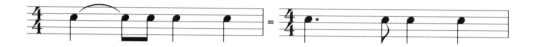

The equivalent note values for a dotted quarter note appears as follows:

A few basic rhythms using dotted notes follow:

Sixteenth-Note Rhythms. Sixteenth-note rhythms are created by dividing the quarter-note beat into four equal parts, or by dividing the eighth-note pulse in half. A sixteenth-note pulse in $\frac{4}{4}$ time would appear as follows:

Play this rhythm, getting a feel for groups of four to the beat, four beats to the bar. Remember to count the beat numbers to yourself (1, 2, 3, 4, and so on). Notice that each beat is isolated by beaming groups of four sixteenth notes. In these more complex rhythms correct use of the beams is very important to help keep track of the beat.

The sixteenth note between a primary beat and an "and" beat is labeled as an "e" beat and the sixteenth note between an "and" beat and the following primary beat is an "a" beat as follows:

1   e   &   a   2   e   &   a   3   e   &   a   4   e   &   a

One interesting way of thinking about sixteenth notes is to isolate a single beat. There are various possibilities for altering the sixteenth note rhythm in one beat. The possibilities will consist of all four sixteenth notes being struck, three out of the four, two of the four, one of the four, or none of the four. Some of them are written below with the primary beats labeled as P. (It may be helpful to repeat each example to yourself several times to let it sink in.)

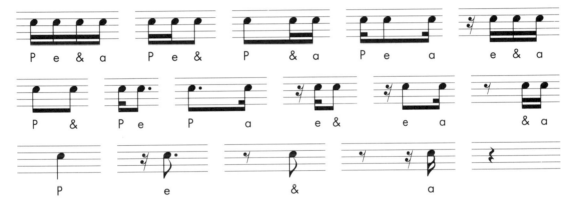

Stringing these beats together in various ways produces a tremendous variety of rhythms:

Create your own rhythms using sixteenth notes. Remember to repeat the rhythms several times when clapping and tapping. Coordinating some of these rhythms can be very tricky at first, so take it slowly and don't be discouraged. It's like learning to ride a bicycle—difficult at first, but easier once you get the hang of it.

Triplet Rhythms. You may have noticed that up to this point all the rhythmic division you've seen has been in multiples of two. The fractional system of notes is based on twos—whole notes, half notes, quarters, eighths, and so on. You have seen groups of three beats in $\frac{3}{4}$ time, but so far we haven't dealt with a situation where beats themselves are divided in three. The notation system uses what is called a "triplet" to create groups of three evenly-spaced notes within a beat. Triplets are notated with a three above the note group, using a bracket if there are no beams. The standard note symbols are used, but as triplets their value is diminished to allow three to the beat—a mathematical anomaly, but used in music nonetheless.

A measure of eighth-note triplets in $\frac{4}{4}$—three evenly spaced notes to the beat—would be labeled and appear as follows:

If you dissect groups of triplets in the same way you did sixteenth notes in the previous section, you can come up with numerous rhythmical possibilities using three, two, one, or no triplets in one quarter-note beat.

You may then create extended triplet rhythms by combining beats from the above possibilities. In the rhythms below notice that there is a tendency to rely on the first and third notes of the triplet (the primary beat and the "ta" beat). This combination of notes is called a shuffle, and it is used extensively in pop music and especially the blues. Notice that the triplet signs help to isolate the individual beats.

Create your own triplet patterns, and rhythms of all types. Remember that rhythms don't always fall into the neat categories covered here. They may combine all of these approaches, including eighth notes, sixteenth notes, and triplets, in the space of a single measure. Most popular music is created from simple combinations such as those you've been practicing so far, but rhythmic invention can stretch much further, and ultimately the possibilities are endless.

4

DRUMS
AND
PERCUSSION

WHEN DEVELOPING RHYTHM PARTS FOR A SONG, or programming rhythm tracks on a drum machine for practice or for recording, it's important to keep two things in mind: the possible beat patterns you can create, and the array of percussion sounds you can use to produce the rhythms. The most important rhythm instrument in today's music is obviously the drum set, which is made up of several types of drums and cymbals. The drum set is used for the basic beats and rhythm patterns of popular music, and current drum machines are geared to reproduce all of its capabilities. But an ever-increasing number of auxiliary instruments are being added to the modern drummer's collection, facilitating the production of a wide range of colors and effects. Many of these instruments are preprogrammed into the sound libraries of drum machines and synthesizers. Before moving on to rhythms in pop music and the technique of operating drum machines, it's a good idea to explore the instruments that have served as the traditional tools of drummers and percussionists, and that continue to provide the basis for today's digitally-generated sounds.

Drums are certainly among the oldest and most widespread of musical instruments. They exist in all parts of the world and come in a staggering number of shapes, sizes, and sounds. The current instruments of the percussion family, including many instruments other than drums, are the products of considerable cross-cultural development and refinement.

The instruments of the percussion family are generally classified into two basic categories: instruments of definite pitch such as the glockenspiel, xylophone, and kettledrum; and instruments of indefinite pitch such as the triangle, bass drum, and tambourine. The second group may be further broken down into hand percussion, meaning instruments held in the hand when played, and the more involved drums and cymbals which require stands or slings. For this discussion we will divide the percussion family into four groups: pitched percussion instruments, hand percussion, drums and cymbals, and the modern drum set.

The techniques for making rhythm are tremendously varied, and involve the use of hands alone or of mallets and sticks. Hand technique may be used on our own bodies, as with "hambone" or certain children's games, or applied directly to a wide variety of instruments such as bongos or tambourine. In the most evolved technique, the use of hands on the Indian *tabla* drum employs a subtle array of gestures which can produce an amazing variety of sounds and pitches. Stick and mallet techniques also vary widely depending on the instrument being played. The military roll on a snare drum, for example, involves a sophisticated stick bouncing technique, while mallet use on the vibraphone, marimba, and related instruments has developed into a complex four-mallet method that allows for chording. We will look at some of these techniques while exploring individual instruments.

Pitched Percussion Instruments. Pitched percussion instruments, not surprisingly, are instruments capable of producing tones recognizable as pitches within the Western system of scales. There are two basic subdivisions within this category. The first is the timpani (often referred to as a kettle drum), which is a large drum played with mallets. The second is a family of instruments loosely based on the piano. While not technically a member of the percussion family, the piano is considered by some to be a rhythm instrument because the striking of its keys is similar to the manner in which most percussion is played (as opposed to the bowing or blowing common to most other orchestral instruments). The instruments based on the piano borrow its keyboard concept but are struck with sticks or mallets rather than with the hand or fingers. We could call these instruments, which include the vibraphone and the marimba, "mallet keyboards." Other cultures use a variety of pitched percussion instruments such as the *entenga* drums of Uganda, the tabla from India, and the increasingly popular steel drums from Trinidad. These are sometimes employed in the popular music of this country.

Timpani consist of a skin (drum head) stretched over a hollow metal shell that is in the shape of a half sphere. Modern timpani may substitute plastic drum heads for skin, and fiberglass shells for copper. The size and resonance of the large shell (23″ to 32″ in diameter) produce a deep, booming tone that is considered pure enough to tune to specific pitches. Tuning is done by tightening or loosening the drum head with screws placed around the rim, or by a pedal attachment which stretches the head more tightly when depressed. Timpani are played with a mallet which consists of a wood or metal handle attached to a globular head that is generally made of felt, though for different effects wood, yarn, leather, plastic, or sponge may also be used.

Set of timpani

A minimum of two timpani are used in most orchestras, and they are normally tuned to the tonic and dominant (the first and fifth pitches of the major or minor scale) in the key of the composition. In twentieth century classical music the role of the timpani has widened, with three or more kettledrums often required, along with frequent changes of tuning during a performance. Timpani are most commonly used for rhythmic accentuation but are also called on to produce sound effects such as thunder. When used in popular music (and it doesn't happen often) timpani can supply quite dramatic accents to highlight or mark the arrival of a particular song section. The Beatles used them in this way to begin the chorus of their 1965 song "Every Little Thing."

Used in pop music quite a bit more frequently than timpani are mallet keyboard instruments: the marimba, the xylophone, and the vibraphone. They provide a light and airy sound that can serve as an effective replacement for keyboard parts in the right song. They can also supply a woody, rustic percussion effect which adds exotic spice to melodies, rhythm, or backing tracks (the Police achieved this effect with a marimba sound in "King of Pain"). These instruments consist of tone bars, made of wood or synthetic material, which are arranged in two rows corresponding to the chromatic scale, just like the white and black keys of the piano. The size and thickness of the tone bars determine the pitch of the note. Below each tone bar is a metal pipe which acts as a resonator. The resonators are tuned to the pitch of the tone bar. They amplify each note and give the tone color a deeper and richer quality.

Marimba

The marimba is an African-based instrument that is played with mallets. It is used primarily for melodies, although chordal harmony can be produced by using two mallets at the same time or by employing the contemporary four-mallet approach (a difficult technique in which two mallets are held in each hand, and are spread out or adjusted to different intervals to play chords). Once a marimba note is played, it decays rapidly. Limited variations in sustain can be achieved by altering the strength of the mallet attack and by muting the note with a free hand. More pronounced sustain can be produced by rapidly alternating mallet attacks on the desired note, resulting in a percussive sustain called "tremolo."

The vibraphone (or vibes) is the most common member of the mallet keyboard family in popular music. From the opening introduction of the Rolling Stones' "Under My Thumb" to the jazz stylings of Milt Jackson, Gary Burton, and Bobby Hutcherson, the vibraphone has long been enjoyed for its distinctive, soft, metallic sound. It differs from the marimba largely in its capacity to produce glowing, sustained notes. This effect is controlled with the use of a pedal that releases felt damping bars from the tone bars, producing sustain. Like the marimba, vibes have a resonator pipe below each tone bar to amplify and enhance the sound of the instrument. The vibraphone, however, also has a mechanical element within each resonator pipe, driven by a small motor attached to the instrument. The motor rotates the element within the resonator pipe, producing a vibrato effect (a minute fluctuation in pitch). The speed of the motor is usually variable, allowing for adjustment in the speed of the vibrato (hence the instrument's name). The combination of a percussive attack and control over sustain and vibrato has made the vibraphone a highly versatile and popular instrument.

Other instruments in the mallet keyboard family that use metal tone bars are the glockenspiel, celesta, orchestra bells, and bell lyra. These are smaller and more primitive instruments than the vibes, having no pedal control over sustain and using either a simple resonator box or no resonators at all. They produce beautifully clear and sustained tones that are appropriate for certain types of music and musical passages. The glockenspiel is well-suited for doubling melody lines, and if you own or obtain a synthesizer or computer program that can produce this sound, you might try to bolster a melody by playing it on the glockenspiel in addition to the original instrument or voice. Bruce Springsteen supposedly stumbled across this technique around the time he was recording the album *Born to Run*, and he has used the sound in songs like "Thunder Road" and "Born to Run," and in his live performances. The celesta is an instrument that has the appearance of a very small piano and is sounded by playing a keyboard. Classical music buffs know of the celesta from its use in "Dance of the Sugar-Plum Fairy," in Tchaikovsky's *Nutcracker Suite*. Another related orchestral instrument is the chimes, essentially a string of resonator pipes which hang and are struck with a leather mallet, producing long, shimmering tones, tuned chromatically to specific pitches. They are often used in jazz or fusion music to add exotic sound effects.

We now turn to instruments described as having indefinite pitch. This doesn't mean that these instruments have no pitch at all, simply that the pitch produced is too complex to categorize within the standard system of scale tones. These instruments do, in fact, have pitch in the sense of sound qualities that can be heard as relatively high or low. The concept of relative pitch is very important in the use of all percussion instruments and has an effect on the way we assign specific rhythm parts to particular drums.

Hand Percussion. Hand percussion could really include thousands of instruments, encompassing "found" objects and everyday tools like spoons and pots, along with traditional instruments such as cowbells and washboards. Some of the recent multi-percussionists like Airto Moreira, Dom Um Romao, and Alejandro Acuna of Weather Report, have elevated the playing of hand percussion to a high art, using a dazzling array of instruments to create infinite shades of musical color. Most popular music, however, draws from a basic collection of hand percussion that includes several traditional Latin-American and African-derived instruments. The following discussion will touch on those instruments that are used most frequently: the triangle, wood block, castanets, whistles, cowbell, claves, tambourine, guiro, maracas and other rattles, and cabasa.

The triangle and the wood block are the simplest forms of hand percussion. The triangle is a simple steel bar, bent in the shape of a triangle and struck with a steel rod. It's suspended from a hook so that it will vibrate freely and produce a high, tinkling sound of indefinite pitch. The wood block is a small block of wood with a thin hollow part just below the top surface which acts as a resonator. The block is struck with a wooden stick to produce a sharp, clacking sound, somewhat like the clopping of horses' hooves. Striking the wood block in different places using either the tip or the side of the stick will produce slight variations in the sound.

Castanets have been widely used by Spanish dancers performing to Flamenco dance music. They consist of two shell-shaped pieces of hard wood which are hinged together with string at their base. The string is looped around the thumb and forefinger of the player's hand allowing the shells to be opened and closed so that they produce a clacking sound. By playing one in each hand, a skillful player of the castanets can produce very rapid and intricate rhythms. Modern orchestral castanets have springs and handles which facilitate playing but eliminate the accuracy of rhythms obtainable with the traditional castanet.

Whistles are used primarily for sound effects, though often the effect is meant for a precise rhythmic location and duration. Some of the sound effects possible from various whistles include birdcalls, sirens, wind sounds, cyclones, and tugboat and train whistles. A whistle may also refer to a small end-blown flute with six finger holes, made of wood, metal, or plastic. Some Brazilian music uses whistles in the context of street samba percussion ensembles.

The cowbell is a metal instrument that has evolved from several sources and is now part of the ever-growing percussion arsenal included in many drum machines. The most traditional type of cowbell contains a clapper and produces a clamorous sound ideally suited to its original use, which was to keep track of the movement of cattle. More recent English and American bells are tuned to definite pitch and are rung in succession to create simple melodies. Today's most commonly used cowbell does not have a clapper and is played with a stick. Like the wood block, the cowbell can produce different sounds depending on where it is struck: at the open end a low tone is sounded; at the closed end a high tone. The volume and piercing quality of the cowbell make it best suited for simple repetitive rhythms, along the lines of its use in the classic Chambers Brothers song, "Time Has Come Today." The cowbell is very common in Latin-American music and Latin-influenced pop tunes.

The word *claves* in Spanish means key to a code or keystone of an arch, which gives some indication of the importance of this percussion instrument in Latin music. It has also crept into rock music: the Beatles, for example, used it prominently in their 1964 hit "And I Love Her." The claves are two cylindrical pieces of hardwood that are struck together, producing a very sharp clacking sound with almost no sustain. The clave sound is often imitated on the drum set, using a technique called "cross-sticking" in which the back end of the drum stick is hit against the rim of the snare drum. This related sound is also included on most popular drum machines under the label "rim."

The word tambourine is derived from the French word for drum, *tambour*. The tambourine is, in fact, a shallow drum, with skin stretched across one side and small metal plates (jingles) attached to the rim. In popular use the tambourine is played much more in the manner of various hand percussion instruments rather than as a drum, with the jingles the predominant aspect of the instrument and the drum head often not played. Some tambourines even omit the head. The tambourine is usually shaken to create a continuous sound, with accents added by tapping on the fist, elbow, or knee. A tambourine with a head may also be played primarily as a drum, with the jingles providing a secondary sound. Intricate patterns can be produced by alternating thumb and fingers on the hand. The tambourine is especially prevalent in Brazilian music, though it is also one of the more widely used percussion instruments in popular music.

A guiro, or scraper, is generally made from a gourd with ribbing carved over most of the outer body. A stick is run over the ribbing producing a scratching sound, with the gourd acting as a resonator. The duration of the sound can be controlled by the length and speed of the hand stroke. The guiro is common in traditional Latin-American and Latin-influenced popular music. The washboard can serve as another kind of scraper and is still used in traditional New Orleans zydeco music, worn hung across the chest and played with both hands.

Maracas are the most common form of a very large class of hand percussion generally described as rattles or shakers. As with the tambourine, rattles are shaken to produce a continuous sound, sometimes accented so that a rhythmic pattern is created. Maracas are dried gourds with a handle, filled with dry seeds or shot. Another kind of common rattle is made from metal tubes filled with pebbles. The sound of a rattle or shaker is frequently included in the library of sounds on drum machines.

A cabasa is sort of a combination of a rattle and a guiro. It is a round gourd rattle with ribbed sides, encased in a network of metal, pebble, or plastic beads. The case of beads is generally held in one hand while the handle of the gourd (or wooden gourd substitute) is held in the other. The beads are scraped and rattled against the gourd with a circular motion of the wrist. Large gourds encased in beads are common in African music and are played by altering the manner of rotating the beads against the gourd, which sometimes includes throwing the gourd rhythmically.

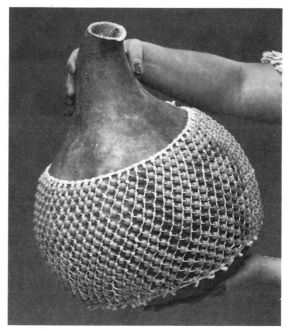

Gourd rattle

There are many other types of hand percussion. Some of them, such as sleigh bells, slapsticks, ratchets, and even anvils, are used to create special sound effects. Still others are wholly human "instruments," and they include hand clapping, finger snapping, patting knees, stamping or scraping feet, and vocal sounds such as grunts, shouts, and breaks in the voice. Hand clapping has become quite widespread in popular music as evidenced by its inclusion in the sound libraries of most drum machines.

All of these instruments can add depth, color, and variety to drum beats and rhythm tracks, and are well worth using in either their "real" or digital form.

Drums and Cymbals. Drums and cymbals, whether used separately or in combination as a drum set, are the central tools of rhythm in most of the world's music, and especially in popular music. Drums have been fashioned into innumerable forms, from makeshift pots to elaborate works of art. The common elements in all drums are the hollow cylinder and the drum head or skin. Drums may have heads on one or both sides, the heads may be tunable (by varying the tautness of the skin over the cylinder), and they may be played either with the hands or with sticks of all different sizes and materials. Cymbals are generally large, circular, primarily brass plates, that are also manufactured or built in various sizes with many different types of sound. They may be struck against each other or played with a stick or sticks. The most commonly used drums and cymbals are the subject of the following discussion.

Bongo and conga drums are probably the most widely used hand drums in the Western hemisphere, and are associated particularly with Latin music. (The name *conga* comes from a Latin dance that was popularized in the United States in the 1940s.) These one-headed drums are either held between the knees (bongos) or placed on the floor (congos). Conga drums are usually played in sets of two, providing a lower and a higher pitch which can generate two-voiced rhythms. Greater tonal variety may be achieved by using additional drums. Three sizes of congas are generally sold today: the tumba (largest size, lowest pitch), the conga (medium size, with the name used generically as well as for this specific sized drum), and the quinta (smallest size, highest pitch).

Conga drum

An enormous number of sounds and pitches may be coaxed from the head of a conga drum. The position of the hand on the drum as well as the shape and part of the hand used (i.e., cupped hand, the palm, the palm and forefinger, the base of the palm) will affect the timbre and the pitch of the sound. A *portamento* (a sliding shift of pitch) effect can be created by sliding or pushing the thumb of one hand across the head while striking the head with the other. Conga drum heads are usually tunable via screws placed around the rim, though more primitive drums with permanently attached heads are tuned by heating and thus stretching the head.

The tom-tom falls into the largest class of drums used in the West. The name tom-tom is derived from the Hindi (Indian) *tamtam*, meaning drum, and has been used to describe American Indian and Oriental drums. Although still defined in Webster's as a hand drum, in current use tom-toms refer to a wide variety of drums that are almost always struck with sticks or mallets. The cylinder of the drum may be made from different types of hard wood, various metal alloys, fiberglass, or other modern synthetic materials. Tom-toms may have one head or two, and the heads are almost always tunable via screws placed around the rim holding the head to the cylinder. The second or bottom head acts as an additional resonator and gives the tom-tom a fuller, rounder sound. Tom-toms are usually found in groups of two or more, varying in diameter, depth, and relative pitch. The tom-toms used in the contemporary drum set are generally of the two-head variety, whereas concert toms (used with an orchestra) have only one head.

Timbales are a high-pitched form of tom-tom with one head. They have a metal shell and are usually played in a pair. Their distinctive sound is created by playing rim shots (using a drum stick to simultaneously strike the rim and the head of the drum), and they are also commonly played on the side of the metal cylinder for a clave-type sound. Timbales are most often used in Latin-American music. Roto toms are a recent invention distinguished by their lack of cylindrical body. The rim, however, may be rotated to tighten or loosen the head, thus allowing for a rapid retuning of the drum. By rotating the rim while striking the drum head, the player can produce a kind of portamento effect.

The snare drum is very much in evidence in current pop music, most often providing a repeating "backbeat" accent that adds tension and interest to the main rhythm. Essentially a kind of tom-tom, the snare drum is a two-head drum with metal, nylon, or catgut strings (called snares) stretched tightly across the bottom head. When the top drum head is struck with a stick the snares vibrate in response, producing a distinctive buzzing or rattling sound. The snare drum also has a release mechanism which frees the snares from the bottom head, allowing the drum to sound like a basic tom-tom.

Snare drum

The snare drum originated as a marching drum used to accompany foot soldiers into battle during the Revolutionary and Civil wars. It still plays a central role in the parade drumming tradition. In this military/marching band context the snare drum is usually played suspended from the drummer's side. But the most common current use of the snare is within the drum set, in which it is placed on a stand.

Stick technique on this drum is especially complex in part because the buzzing of the snares serves to stretch out or sustain the sound. Certain playing techniques, originally used in the military, allow for unique special effects. One of these is the "military roll," which is carried out by rapidly bouncing the two sticks in alternation on the top head of the drum. The quickly repeating beats generate a continuous buzzing sound from the snares.

A standard set of snare drum rudiments was developed in the 1930s, and they are still used today in elementary drum education. There are thirteen standard drum rudiments and a total of twenty-six rudiments in the basic approach to the snare drum. The rudiments include various basic rolls and alternating stick combinations such as the five- and seven-stroke rolls. Other rudiments have names that suggest their sound on their required hand movement, such as in the examples below.

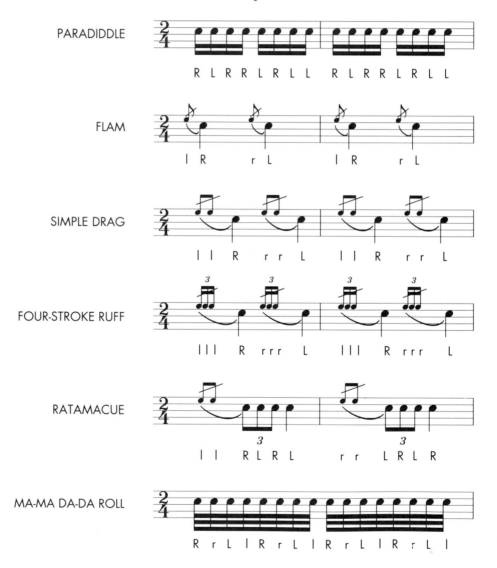

By combining various rudiments the drummer can create many different sounds and rhythms, most of which we recognize from the military drum tradition. Some of these rudiments, especially the flam (which is really just a grace note) are also common in popular drum set rhythms. The slurs created in the drag or ruff, in which several grace notes (created by bouncing the stick) precede an accented note, are also common in popular technique. Although the bounces are distinct in number (two in a drag, three in a four-stroke ruff, and so on) the effect is the same: a continuous rattle of the snares preceding the struck note. It is a sound which, of course, is unique to the snare drum.

Tenor drums and bass drums are larger members of the tom-tom family. Both are used in parade drumming, and are generally suspended from the body with straps and played with sticks or mallets. The bass drum is carried upright and struck on both sides with either hand. Both of these instruments have adapted to the drum set, with the tenor drum put on legs and called the floor tom, and the bass drum placed upright on the floor and played with a foot pedal.

Cymbals offer a bright contrast to the sound of drums, and in the context of rock and pop rhythms they've been put to a number of uses. In general, cymbals consist of large circular plates, usually made from a predominantly brass alloy. They are made in a very wide variety of sizes and shapes, from very large and heavy gongs that are struck with mallets to small finger cymbals that are played similarly to castanets. Most cymbals are quite thin and range from 10" to 24" in diameter. In the more traditional methods of performance, cymbals are played in pairs of equal-sized plates, with straps attached to the center of the cymbals so they may be held and struck together, producing a clashing sound. Cymbals may also be suspended individually and struck with a variety of types of sticks. In a drum set they are placed in numerous positions, on floor stands, and on holders that are attached to certain drums.

Stick technique, meaning the grip and manipulation of the drum sticks or mallets, varies depending on the style of music and the type of instrument you're playing. The basic technique involves holding the stick between the end of the thumb and the first joint of the forefinger, with the back of the stick running across the palm. This is similar to the way we would hold a hammer, except that the thumb is held against the stick. The stick may also be held more loosely, with the play of the stick in the hand controlled by the ring and pinky fingers. The degree of play in the stick, as well as the position and tightness of the grip, will differ according to the musical style. In the last few decades some drummers have developed quite intricate finger techniques that allow for very rapid rhythms and grace notes.

Traditional military drumming requires a different grip for the left hand stick. This traditional grip has the stick held at the base of the left-hand thumb and forefinger with the end of the stick protruding through the fingers, much as we normally hold a pen or pencil but with the wrist held up rather than down. This grip allows easy access to a drum when it is hanging at an angle from the side of a marching drummer.

A "matched grip" is one in which both hands are using the "hammer" type of grip described above. It has been the most widely used stick grip in today's music because of its application to the drum set, which has eclipsed the marching/military drum tradition. The matched grip is also used with orchestra percussion and mallet percussion instruments.

The Drum Set. The modern drum set is a marvel of ingenuity and practicality. It draws together a number of percussion instruments and borrows a basic structural concept from the piano: that the feet as well as the hands can be used to expand the musician's control of the instrument. By adding foot pedals to a practical configuration of assorted drums and cymbals, it brings to the single player the ability to produce many simultaneous rhythms and varying sound qualities. Its usefulness and range have made it the central percussion instrument in popular music.

The drum set evolved over several decades, and was made possible in part by manufacturing techniques developed around the turn of the century. The invention of the bass drum pedal by George Olney in 1887 provided an initial mechanical breakthrough. It transferred from the hands to the feet the act of striking the bass drum with a mallet, and then freed the hands for other drum or percussion tasks.

A similar result was achieved by the development of the hi-hat, a vital component of the modern drum set. The hi-hat consists of a stand and foot pedal with two cymbals attached. The cymbals are facing each other in the manner of orchestra or parade cymbals that are struck together. By pressing the foot pedal, the drummer can cause the cymbals to strike each other, thus accomplishing a musical task that at one time had required two hands.

The height of the cymbals makes it possible to play them with sticks, which can be done while the cymbals are open or closed. In the open position a splashy sustained sound is produced, the duration of which can be precisely controlled by altering the tension on the foot pedal, or which can be choked off completely. In the closed position a very clipped cymbal sound is produced, now widely used as the "ride" part of drum patterns. Open and closed hi-hat sounds are commonly included in the library of sounds on most drum machines.

The hi-hat began as a hand-operated instrument that used a spring to close the cymbals together. It could be played with one hand, freeing the other hand to perform a different function. This instrument was used in the early 1920s to accompany the Charleston, a popular dance of the time. The rhythm had a "boom/chick" sound produced by playing a rim shot on the drum on beat 1 followed by a cymbal clash on beat 2. This basic two-beat rhythm—a forerunner of the modern backbeat—could be performed by a single percussionist playing a rim shot with one hand and the hand-held cymbals with the other.

The first operation of two cymbals with a foot pedal accompanied the introduction of the low-hat, or low-boy, in 1923. The cymbals were low to the ground and had the appearance of a top hat, thereby inspiring the name. In 1928 Barney Walberg attached the low-hat to a thirty-two-inch tube, creating the modern hi-hat.

Beginning around the turn of the century, and continuing through the mid-1920s, makeshift drum sets were assembled by individual percussionists using all manner of assorted drum and percussion items. The demand for multipercussion sounds came partly from vaudeville theater and the silent movies, which needed accompanying sound effects for the films and back-up drumming for the musical acts that performed while projectionists changed reels. The name "trap drums"—a slang term for the drum set that is still in use—came from a shortening of the word "contraptions." (One can imagine a theater owner asking a percussionist to bring his "drums and contraptions" down to the theater to accompany the shows.)

By the 1930s the modern drum set had more or less settled into a standard combination of the two pedal instruments (the bass drum and the hi-hat), a snare drum on a stand, and a hanging cymbal (ride cymbal) placed on a stand so that it could be played with a stick. The addition of a tom-tom (or tom-toms) mounted on the bass drum, and another tom-tom with legs placed on the floor (floor tom), completed the basic drum set as shown below:

Drum set

This configuration has remained intact for the past half century. The only changes have focused on improvement of the pedal design and structural hardware, and the addition and refinement of drums and cymbals. The most notable additions have been assorted tom-toms and more hanging cymbals of different sizes and varieties.

The basic drum stick has also remained much the same over this period of time. The drum stick is 15″ to 17″ long, tapering to a beaded tip (modern drum stick tips are often nylon rather than wood, because they are more durable). Mallets and brushes (wire brushes on the end of sticks) are occasionally used to produce special effects.

The basic assignment of hands and feet to components of the drum set, for a right-handed person, is as follows: the right foot operates the bass drum pedal; the left foot operates the hi-hat pedal; the right hand uses a stick to play one of the hanging cymbals or the hi-hat cymbals; the left hand uses a stick to play the snare drum. The two hands also work together to create rolls, fills, and other "breaks" or short connecting rhythms, usually played on the snare drum and tom-toms.

Although the specifics of drum techniques may vary, the fundamental idea is to create rhythms within the statement of the pulse. The individual components of the drum set have specific functions that support this concept. The hi-hat and ride cymbal are pulse-oriented, while the snare and bass drums are used for rhythm. If approached from the perspective of a right-handed drummer, the task of time-keeping is assigned to the strongest and weakest limbs (the right hand on the ride pattern and the left foot on the hi-hat pedal) and the rhythm function is carried out by the left hand on the snare and the right foot on the bass drum:

right hand = ride pattern (on cymbals) = pulse keeping
right foot = bass drum = downbeat + rhythm
left hand = snare drum = backbeat + rhythm
left foot = hit-hat pedal = slower pulse keeping

The basic concept of maintaining a pulse in one's strongest limb (right hand) and weakest limb (left foot) reflects the drummer's primary role as time-keeper.

The logic by which instrument frequency ranges are matched to rhythmic function also seems to support the idea of the importance of the pulse. One of the pulse-keeping instruments is the hi-hat, which generates frequencies that are high enough to keep it out of the way of most other instruments and voices. The all-important downbeat, along with other fundamental points of rhythmic resolution, is sounded in the low frequency range of the bass drum, which also provides varying degrees of rhythmic development. The snare drum, operating in the middle frequencies, provides the backbeat, which is the fundamental rhythmic statement in most contemporary musical styles. The tom-toms, also in the middle frequencies, are used for embellishment and to fill in spaces allocated for rhythm statements. We can think of the high frequencies of the cymbals as providing a counterpoint to the low-sounding bass drum and the insistent backbeat of the snare.

These drumming procedures are meant only to provide a framework for understanding, and are not to be taken as unbendable rules; sometimes the exceptions to the rules provide the most interesting and power-ful musical statements. Within the more progressive offshoots of rock and roll, funk, and jazz, there are plenty of exceptions to the basic pulse-keeping or rhythm-making functions assigned to particular drums. Now, with the arrival of new digital instruments and drum machines, the logic of drum set rhythm is no longer linked with physical dexterity and the assignment of strong limbs to prominent drum beats. The creation of rhythm patterns is now subject only to the whim, ear, and artistic judgment of the instrument user—the new rhythmist. Now, more than ever, that creative judgment needs a point of reference from which to move in new and innovative directions. It is only by examining the accepted practices in current pop music and its root forms that the creative drummer can make informed decisions about what possible new directions to take.

PART TWO

THE ROOTS
OF MODERN
RHYTHM

5
A BRIEF
HISTORY
OF RHYTHM

JUST AS RHYTHM PROVIDES the essential underpinning of today's popular songs, linking the music with the most common of human actions, from the heartbeat to dance, work, and play, so have pop rhythms grown and developed over the years into a diverse collection of styles and approaches. On one end of the spectrum you find basic rock beats, anchored by simple bass drum downbeats, sparked by snare accents, and held in place by the hi-hat pulse. On the other end are highly developed funk rhythms, heavily syncopated and colored by an array of special effects and electronic sounds. The rhythms are different, and yet they share certain common elements, all traceable to the original formulas from which the styles have grown. The rhythm approaches heard today on the radio and performed in many types of bands represent only the most recent stages of a series of evolutionary steps going back decades and even centuries.

For the new rhythm player who is on the cutting edge of developments in music and instrumentation, and who is involved in creating drum beats for original music, it is helpful to go back and connect with the old—with the traditions that have laid the groundwork for current and future sounds. The cliché "there is nothing new under the sun" might raise the hackles of some artists who stand by the pure originality of their work, but in the final analysis, current art couldn't exist without the preparation of previous history and preceding artworks. Every new creation is in some way a synthesis of what has come before—a blending and intermingling of old ideas that, when approached from a new perspective and interpreted in a new voice, are broadened and turned into something fresh and original. This has certainly been true in the development of pop music, with interpretations of blues and country, for example, yielding the hybrid form of rock and roll.

Rhythm itself, as used in the pop music we play and listen to today, is ultimately the result of two converging traditions: the European "classical" practices from which we also draw much of our harmony, melody, and sense of form; and African folk idioms and ideas, which have brought to American music the vital elements of spontaneity and syncopated rhythmic freedom. Let's examine the two traditions separately and then look at how their convergence has shaped the diverse rhythms in current popular use.

Tracing the Western Tradition. Rhythm in the Western tradition ("Western" meaning essentially the European classical forms) has not served a pronounced central role in the sense of prominent rhythm instruments used to set up a beat.

The concept of rhythm has instead been tied in closely with the idea of melodic motion, of the duration of notes, and of the rate and flow of their movement. So to discuss rhythm in this tradition, we also have to discuss melody.

Prior to the twelfth century the primary form of music in the Western classical tradition was apparently monophonic, or music consisting of a single melodic line without additional harmony or accompaniment. It is generally referred to as "plainsong," and is the style both of Greek music and of Gregorian chant. The music probably stretched from non-rhythmical to rhythmically regular and from non-melodic and monotonous to quite complex. Gregorian chant is generally conceded to have had considerable rhythmic freedom, though scholars still debate the exact rhythmic nature of most early forms of music. It was with the rise of polyphony and more elaborate musical forms that we can really begin to trace rhythm through history to the present.

Polyphony means "many sounds" and refers to the simultaneous use of two or more melodic lines, each with individual significance and independence. Polyphony didn't really begin to develop until the middle of the twelfth century, though there were some indications of earlier uses. The first proliferation of measured rhythm occurred from c. 1150 to c. 1250 with the use of "rhythmic modes." These modes developed into the system called "mensural rhythm," which was the precursor of the modern system.

Early polyphony required rhythmical organization, and the rhythmic modes set up a very basic system. The modes consisted of short rhythmic phrases that were combined to create extended rhythms. They were made up of combinations of two lengths of tones, long and short. These rhythmic patterns were used more or less consistently in polyphonic composition, with each individual part adhering to one mode. Two simple melodies with simple, repeating rhythms were played independently, or as we would say today, in counterpoint.

During this period, units of three were considered to be "perfect" time and all of the modes were grouped in time measures of three beats. Triple time dominated the musical world, though duple time was also in occasional use. Written in modern notation the rhythms that created the six commonly known rhythm modes of this time are shown below:

During much of the polyphonic period, c. 1260 to c. 1600, a different and more complete system of duple and triple meter came into use, called mensural rhythm (meaning "measured rhythm"). This system was necessitated by growth in rhythmic complexity and in greater use of duple meter.

Mensural rhythm differed in notation from the modern form in that it contained no bar lines, no ties, and no triplets. Rather than using triplets it used perfect and imperfect forms of notes, a holdover from the modes. Below are shown the original forms of mensural rhythm:

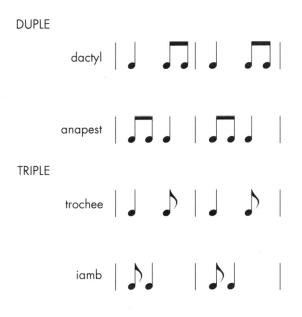

Theoretically, mensural rhythm is meter without stress, as heard in the almost stressless flow of Renaissance polyphony. Subsequent mensural rhythms, however, required accents as in the meters below:

Eventually, meter and time signature became linked, and meter became an underlying rhythm rather than the actual played or sung rhythm.

The Baroque period, c. 1600 to c. 1750, saw a shift from polyphonic to homophonic music, and from mensural rhythm to the modern system. The advent of monody, music for a single singer with accompaniment, marked this turning point. As polyphonic music was abandoned and accompanied melody introduced, rhythms became subordinate to melody. The simple and strong body rhythms of the Baroque period were indicative of the association of most of this music with dance, just as today's pop music is closely associated with dance.

Homophonic music, referring to a single melody line supported by chords or other subordinate material, has been the dominant form in Western music from 1600 to the present (though there has been a renewed interest in polyphony in this century). Homophonic music generally makes less of a demand on the listener than does polyphony. With the development of homophonic music, rhythm evolved into the modern metrical system, based on time signature and meter rather than on repeating rhythms previously called meters.

The Rococo period, from c. 1710 to c. 1775, emphasized pleasantness and prettiness in a similar fashion to the art of the day and in contrast to the seriousness and dignity of Baroque. In general, the newfound use of harmony in seventeenth and eighteenth century music tended to limit rhythmic subtleties and flexibility in the use of stress accents. While conforming to our modern notions of meter, music of this period was rhythmically very simple.

The same was true of the Classical period, roughly bounded by the years 1750 to 1820. Although marked by great and enduring pieces of music, the Classical period retained most of the rhythmic simplicity and metric constraints of the earlier styles.

The Romantic period occupied most of the nineteenth century, and, while progressing through several stages, extended the freedom of rhythm and meter within attempts to achieve powerfully emotional expression. A significant rhythmic development was the use of syncopation, beginning in the late works of Beethoven. While syncopation was found in some fourteenth century French music, it was largely absent from the Western tradition until the Romantic period. Syncopation and other advanced rhythmic concepts didn't occupy a central place in Western music until music from other cultures—notably Africa—began to exert a stronger influence in the West.

An interesting aspect of the development of music during this period is the change that occurred in musical practice after around 1850. Up until that time, musicians were naturally composers and improvisers as well as interpreters of other people's music. Keyboard players would improvise accompaniments based on written numbers called "figured bass." After 1850, composing became a specialized skill. The ability of classical musicians to learn by ear and to improvise has greatly diminished since that time. In popular music the ability to play by ear, to improvise, and to compose may be more integrally combined, as they were prior to 1850. Some contemporary classical musicians have looked to popular music as a means of rediscovering and developing these essential musical skills.

In the twentieth century there has been a tremendous acceleration in the development of rhythm in Western music. Much of this development, beginning with the primitivistic rhythms of early twentieth century composers, has come from cross-cultural and popular forms of music. In general the line between "popular" and "classical" forms has blurred and many amalgamations of musical styles have appeared within various contexts. Lively Slavic dance rhythms and the complex syncopations of jazz have been very influential in much of contemporary music. Within jazz itself, where rhythmic syncopation is often referred to as the hallmark of the musical form, rhythms and rhythmic formats have developed greatly.

Though classical music has borrowed heavily from popular and non-Western forms, its own profound impact can be measured in terms of the most basic, widely accepted concepts such as the homophonic structure of music (simple melody with harmony). It has also produced pioneers in the field of electronic music and new technology. The use of electronic instruments, computers, and non-musical sounds—an active part of contemporary music-making—were first explored by classical composers like Pierre Boulez, Karlheinz Stockhausen, and John Cage.

6
THE
AFRICAN
CONNECTION

PERHAPS THE MOST FASCINATING ASPECT of rhythm's evolution has been the introduction of African-derived approaches into the Western tradition. We can hear it in modern dance music from Madonna to Run-DMC, in jazz and blues, and in rock and roll. The African influence is present in nearly every phase of pop music: in the improvisation of vocalists, jazz musicians, rock guitarists, and all kinds of drummers; in the "call and response" structure of back-up singers echoing lead vocalists, and of snare backbeats answering bass drum pulses; in the "blue notes" that are the melodic centerpieces of rock and jazz; in the syncopation that lifts standard four-four rhythm to more catchy levels of tension and interest; in the inflection and voice-like sounds of instruments, including some of the electronic drums in current use; and in the "swing" feel of accenting and shifting beats, of stating musical ideas obliquely and indirectly rather than directly and on-the-beat. These elements are such an intrinsic part of the way we hear and play music that we're often not aware of them at all.

Before tracing the flow of African rhythm into the vast mainstream of American pop, it's valuable to examine the significant features of the African tradition before it interacted with the West.

The African Tradition. In the music of Africa, the drum is as central an element as the piano and violin are in the Western classical tradition. Rhythm plays the primary musical role, just as melody does in European practice.

The drum—as the central tool—is augmented with batteries of all kinds of percussion instruments. (African drums and percussion instruments are cousins of the Latin-American percussion instruments described in the last chapter.) The talking drum, vital in traditional West African forms and still used prominently in popular cross-cultural African bands, is one of the few instruments from the African arsenal that did not later take root in Latin and South America.

Modern talking drum

The talking drum appears in a variety of sizes and shapes. The pitch of the drum is stretched up by pulling the cord (or a handle in modern versions) attached to the center of the drum head. Through intricate interactions between striking and stretching the head the player can produce remarkable voice-like sounds, inflections, and melodies. The infinitely flexible sound of the talking drum places it at the opposite end of the spectrum from many electronic drum machines, with their essentially synthetic, rigid timbres. It embodies the element of "feel" in rhythm.

The vocal quality of this instrument points to the purpose and use of rhythm in African society. Folk music expresses unspoken versions of stories, proverbs, and legends. The drums tell the stories, with specific rhythms communicating different parts of the narrative. Music is also a central part of formal and informal functions, and is used to announce births and deaths, to mark arrivals and departures (especially for hunting), to find lost children, and to teach the young about the environment. In the African tradition, playing an instrument is an extension of signing, bringing vocal nuance, inflection, and ambiguity of tone to an instrument.

Rhythm and inflection are, in many ways, the strongest distinguishing elements of African music. Both elements may be applied broadly, with rhythmic complexity evident in melody as well as accompaniment, and inflection relating to both rhythmic and tonal aspects of music.

Traditional African melody employs dissonance and tones of indeterminate pitch. The dissonance occurs in the combination of melodic parts, as there is no harmony in the Western chordal sense. The secondary melodies—or countermelodies to the main theme—often take the form of repeated short motifs that are sung or played, similar to what is sometimes called a "riff" in blues or jazz. The dissonance frequently takes the form of the "blue notes" of jazz—the flatted third, fifth, and seventh.

Another prominent part of African melody is antiphony (from the Greek *antiphonia* or "counter sound"). Antiphony refers to the "call and response" vocal format in which a phrase is sung, followed by an answer phrase. The call and response may be carried out by a soloist and a chorus, or by two choruses. The phrases may overlap and become quite elaborate.

A key element of music in Africa, and one that is also found in early Western traditions, is improvisation. African music is improvisational on all levels of rhythm and melody within a complex and rigorous discipline, whether sung or played on an instrument.

These basic elements of the African tradition have had an enormous impact on popular music in the West, although in their integrated form they are far different from the way they were in their original setting. Whole aspects of African music, such as the folklore forms that communicate elaborate messages through specific rhythms, have not been absorbed into Western music. Our examination of these concepts will focus on their current structure and makeup as they have become used in the West, not as they exist in traditional African music. But before looking at and learning to play some of these borrowed rhythmic elements, let's follow the flow of African music to the West, and into the familiar styles that we've been playing and listening to for decades.

The Tradition Comes West. The slave trade from Africa to the West in the eighteenth and nineteenth centuries brought certain cultural gifts along with its legacy of suffering and injustice. It is a testament to the strength and vitality of African music and culture that, in spite of its being uprooted, transplanted, and suppressed, many of its basic elements were able to survive and flourish in a new and foreign setting.

The slaves came primarily from the western coast of Africa, though they were also brought from central, southern, and eastern sections. Under English and American subjugation they were taken to the islands of the Caribbean and to the east coast of North America. Under the Portuguese and the Spanish they were sent to Brazil and Venezuela. Though slave customs differed greatly in these far-flung settings, there remain striking similarities in the survival of the musical culture.

In Latin America and the Caribbean the music of the displaced Africans was allowed free expression. African traditions took hold and began exerting widespread influence in popular and dance music. They are most clearly identifiable in the music of Haiti, which exhibits a direct link to African sources, and in the Afro-Cuban tradition through its extraordinarily complex rhythm patterns and instrumental timbres used in song and dance accompaniment.

In contrast to the ease with which African influence blended with Latin-American practices, those same influences were slow to come into North American popular music. Part of the reason was that slaves were commonly prohibited from dancing, drumming, and pursuing other forms of musical expression. In Joseph Conrad's *Heart of Darkness*, the drums beat when "the natives were restless," and in the United States drumming came to symbolize the culture that the white man intended to eradicate in the name of enlightened progress. (Drumming, of course, had been integrated into all aspects of African cultures and represented far more than expressions of aggression.) Still, African music managed to develop in various locations in the American South, and ultimately followed a circuitous—though not well-documented—route into American music.

Among the musical forms that grew out of the Southern fields and plantations were spirituals, West African work songs, and field hollers. The latter two are cited as being precursors to country blues, which, along with black religious music, became a root form of American pop. Each of these combined African concepts with elements drawn from the European harmonic tradition. The black spiritual, which borrowed harmony from English Protestant hymns, also rested on a "call and response" relationship between the vocal soloist and an answering chorus, as well as African approaches to syncopation and vocal timbre. The blues, while resting firmly on a European I-IV-V chord structure, also exhibited a call and response form in the tendency of vocal lines to be answered by guitar lines. Both spirituals and blues employed the African-based element of improvisation.

Although the specific locations of pop music origin are open to debate, New Orleans proved to be a seeding ground of particular importance, especially with regard to the birth of the popular instrumental tradition. At the start of the nineteenth century, New Orleans was evenly divided between the French and the Spanish on the one hand, and the Africans on the other. The lines of demarcation between the two cultures were not rigidly drawn. Both Catholicism and Vodun, a religion derived from African ancestor worship, were practiced by all races. The overall outlook was permissive, due to the "melting pot" nature of the New Orleans population and the city's role as a prosperous port and a center of trade. The drum was never banned in Louisiana, nor was dancing prohibited.

The intermingling of races, culture, and musical traditions made New Orleans a prime site for the early growth of jazz. A movement of consequence in jazz development, linked to the city's affinity for all things French, was its enthusiastic adoption of Napoleon's favored ensemble, the military band. The "negro marching bands" that evolved from the concept of the military band were first used to provide music at funerals. By the mid-nineteenth century they were so popular that they were hired for all kinds of functions by all segments of New Orleans society. These bands employed improvisation, call and response, and other musical practices brought from Africa, which, though foreign to most of the listeners, were mixed with sufficiently traditional elements to be widely accepted.

Smaller combinations of these brass bands began to play for dancers in places of entertainment in New Orleans. It was in Storyville, the famed red light district in the turn-of-the-century French Quarter, that the jazz pianist came into being, playing in a style that was later to be called boogie-woogie. An early form of syncopated music called ragtime developed, and the accompanying dance—the cakewalk—created a controversial sensation. (Although ragtime was hailed by some as America's new music, it was also condemned as vulgar, suggestive, and un-American.) Along with syncopated rhythms, ragtime used European harmonies and elements of the John Philip Sousa marches that were the most popular music of the day. When Storyville was closed down in 1917, many of the unemployed jazzmen traveled up the Mississippi to Kansas City and Chicago, both of which became centers of jazz and blues.

The country blues style, consisting of solo vocalist with acoustic guitar accompaniment, had spread from its Southern origins in the early twentieth century and provided the foundation for later "classic" blues performances of singers backed by full bands. Recordings by popular vocalists such as Ma Rainey and Bessie Smith brought national recognition to the music in the 1920s.

In the Northern cities, the blues later began to take an electric slant, combining amplified guitars and harmonies with keyboard, bass, and drums. Urban blues bands proliferated during the 30s and 40s, yielding a number of national hits.

A further development of the blues, called rhythm and blues, blended gospel/shout vocals with blues harmonies and rhythms drawn from swing and boogie-woogie. Originally promulgated in the late '30s and '40s by jump bands like Louis Jordan's Tympany Five and the Harlem Hamfats, rhythm and blues eventually laid the groundwork for rock and roll under the high-energy stylings of Little Richard and Fats Domino. Elvis Presley blended it with country sounds in the mid-'50s, yielding an early rock-and-roll precursor called rockabilly. And all of these styles retained the shouting vocal inflection, syncopated rhythm, call-and-response voice/instrument patterns, and improvisation that stemmed from African culture's entry into the West.

In the '60s R&B split off into two directions. The first was soul music, heavily dependent on the smooth vocal approach of former gospel singers like Sam Cooke and Clyde McPhatter. As the style grew in popularity, along with artists like Marvin Gaye, Stevie Wonder, The Temptations, The Supremes, Otis Redding, and Aretha Franklin, the rhythms grew more refined, streamlining the rough-hewn swing/shuffle/boogie-woogie beats of earlier days into smooth, propulsive, pop underpinnings. The second offshoot was funk, a flashier, more exciting form that evolved from the stop-on-a-dime precision of James Brown's band through the gospel/rock/funk/psychedelic anthems of Sly and the Family Stone. Both styles metamorphosed in the '70's: soul into the rhythmically homogeneous, studio-slick disco; funk into more of the funky same, aided, abetted, and refined by the addition of synthesized percussion and new "slap" bass techniques.

White rock musicians drew from the blues/R&B tradition as well. Much of the Beatles' early popularity stemmed from their regurgitations of Little Richard tunes and black U.S. rhythms, while the Stones enjoyed similar success by borrowing from Chuck Berry and other blues-based artists. In the late '60s a number of white players and bands locked on to Chicago blues and hammered it into a fiery, virtuosic form that paved the way for hard rock and heavy metal. Among these artists were Eric Clapton, Jimmy Page, Jeff Beck, Fleetwood Mac, and Canned Heat.

Jazz, meanwhile, had undergone another set of changes subsequent to the early days of ragtime, boogie-woogie, and brass bands. As the music spread to various urban centers in the first part of this century, the styles expanded, blended in with other approaches, and coalesced into new forms. Among them was "swing" music. Though swing is broadly defined as an approach to performance encompassing particular rhythmic variations, it also refers to the style of jazz that dominated the 1930s, played by numerous big bands and small groups. The "time shifting" aspect of swing was further refined in the 1940s with the clamorous arrival of bebop. Kenny Clarke, Max Roach, Elvin Jones, and other drummers in this style stretched out the syncopation factor until an entirely new rhythm was implied, drawing jazz drumming ever closer to polyrhythm. The impact of swing and bebop drumming has stayed with jazz ever since, providing the model approach from which further explorations into syncopation, polyrhythm, and free rhythm have been launched.

Fueled by the combined force of these stylistic elements, current pop music (jazz inclusive) continues to expand and develop while maintaining fully integrated and refined versions of well-established rhythmic/harmonic concepts. The traditions that are at the root of today's forms and approaches were virtually unknown in the West prior to the turn of the century.

Again, it is a tribute to the strength of the musical concepts that they have exerted such an important influence in such a relatively short period of time. Some of them are now absolutely central to virtually all styles of popular music. Let's take a closer look at those concepts that are most important to pop rhythm.

Syncopation and the Backbeat. The widespread use of syncopation in popular music today is primarily the result of influences from other cultures, especially African. As defined in Chapter Three, syncopation is any abnormality in meter, such as an accented beat on a normally unaccented beat. By extending syncopation throughout a piece of music one can effectively create a new meter, or a new underlying sense of accentuation. It is a form of "abnormal" meter, or syncopation, that yields one of the cornerstones of pop music: the backbeat.

Listen to almost any pop song and you'll hear it. The now immortalized "backbeat, you can't lose it"—also called "fatback"—has provided current music with a catchy, offbeat hook and has brought about an essential shift in the way rhythm feels. In the Western classical tradition rhythm is smooth and flowing, in support of melody and harmony. In music with a backbeat, rhythm adopts a new internal logic; it has a built-in tension, a constantly recurring suspension and release. The use of the backbeat has changed the way we respond to rhythm while increasing the overall importance of rhythmic feel to the music.

The backbeat refers to accents placed on beats 2 and 4, answering "back" to the normally accented beats 1 and 3 in $\frac{4}{4}$ meter. The backbeats may be obviously stated, as they usually are in popular music, or they may be subtly felt, as is more common in traditional African music. In either case, they do not supercede beats 1 and 3 but interact with them to create an internal form of call and response. The measure is rhythmically centered on beat 1 (the primary resolution); by accenting beat 2 we provide an answer or response to the feeling of arrival on beat 1. This action is repeated with beat 3 (the secondary resolution) and the beat 4 response. Examine the following diagram and compare it to the traditional $\frac{4}{4}$ meter shown on page 35.

D = downbeat
/ = accented beat (backbeat)
– = secondary accent (secondary downbeat)

In most popular music this relationship is expressed by bass drum hits on beats 1 and 3, answered by the snare drum on 2 and 4.

To focus on the difference in feel between the backbeat rhythm and the traditional Western approach, consider the following question: If an audience is clapping along with a band, which beats do they clap on? A classically trained audience, or one that is unfamiliar with rock and pop rhythm, is likely to clap on beats 1 and 3 (even though the band and the snare drum are pushing the backbeat). A typical jazz or gospel audience will clap on beats 2 and 4, feeling these accents as an essential response to beats 1 and 3. Even though the backbeat is completely integrated into popular music, the audience, and even the musicians, may not have fully integrated it into the way they feel the pulse.

Experiment with clapping or tapping your foot along with music that you're familiar with. Try clapping on all four beats, then just on beats 1 and 3, then try clapping only on beats 2 and 4 (the backbeat). When clapping on the backbeat we still feel 1 and 3 as strong beats, with the backbeat providing a response to them. This adds up to a much more involved approach to pulse-keeping than is employed in traditional music: The backbeat is already featured prominently in popular music, yet our response to it and feel for it will vary.

Accent and Swing. Accentuation, whether applied to the backbeat or to other beats, has been used widely in popular music. The importance of accenting in determining sound quality, and the way its use differs in pop and classical music, is illustrated in a basic saxophone technique. In blues-based music, sax players tend to tongue every note (use their tongue on the reed at the start of the note to produce a strong attack). In classical music the sax player plays most notes *legato* (flowing from one note to the other without attacking each one.) The sax player who tongues every note has the ability to provide varying degrees of accent to most of the notes played. He is using accent and inflection to enhance the vocal quality of his instrument. The following examples apply accenting to simply rhythms to produce syncopation. The > indicates an accented note. Notice that these rhythms all include the backbeat accents, and the last two rhythms are further syncopated in their omission of beat 3.

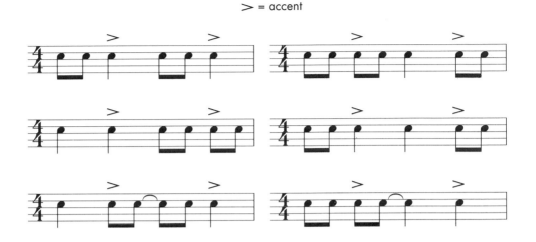

More systematic manipulations of accent and inflection lead to the concept of "swing." Although swing has been used to define a particular style of jazz, it refers most often to an approach to playing in which the placement of notes is shifted slightly in relationship to the beat. This is often described as playing "in front of the beat" or "behind the beat." Put differently, the attack of a given note may be placed slightly before or after the mathematically proper place relative to the pulse, yielding a looser, more syncopated feeling. A consistent pattern of this kind of manipulation is a prominent feature of jazz, and it makes it nearly impossible to notate the music exactly as it should be played. For this reason, the swing factor in a given piece of written music is often indicated by a verbal instruction at the top of the score. New technology, as discussed later in this book, has made it much easier to record and analyze the subtle nuances of the swing feel.

Polyrhythm. Polyrhythm, like syncopation, is a broad musical concept that may be applied in numerous ways. In the most general sense, polyrhythm is the simultaneous use of rhythms which do not agree in subdivision and/or meter. As you will see, this may take a variety of forms which vary in use and complexity.

Polyrhythm, in its simplest form, may be described as an extension of syncopation and phrasing. If we extend some of the basic concepts of syncopation that were shown in Chapter Three we may produce a very simple polyrhythm. By playing consistently on the off beat (the "and" beats that divide the primary beats), we briefly establish the feeling of a new pulse, offset from the underlying beat. This new pulse suggests an alternative beat, disconnected from, though related to, the primary beat. As discussed previously, this may be called a cross-pulse.

P = primary beat (in this example sounded only on the 1 beat of the first measure)
A = alternate beat (in this example sounded in between each primary beat)

We can also create a polyrhythm by using rhythmic phrases made up of note groups other than the usual numerical divisions of the time signature. In the following one-bar examples, the rhythm is phrased in three-beat groups. The effect is that of superimposing a three-beat cycle over a two-beat pulse. The rhythm has two groups of three and then a final group of two, completing the eight-beat cycle of the measure. Count this rhythm in four with accents, then try counting it as two groups of three and a group of two. The curved lines indicate the natural phrasing.

Sometimes a polyrhythmic effect is created by the interaction of many syncopated lines, even though no obvious counter-phrase, such as the one above, is used. The overall effect is of many rhythms and phrases suggesting all kinds of contrary beat groups and meters. This is especially common in jazz and in other improvised settings.

Another kind of polyrhythm expands on the simple use of phrasing to produce cross-pulses. The two most common kinds of cross-pulses, two against three and three against two, are called hemiola. Hemiola is the term for note values standing in relationship of three to two. What then is the difference between two against three and three against two? The ultimate effect is similar; the difference lies in getting there. Both of these rhythms are implied in two basic components of the notational system: the dotted note and the triplet. As you shall see, the dotted note arrives at hemiola by superimposing a two pulse over a previously established three;

the triplet fits a three pulse over a preset two. Let's explore this further.

We'll begin in $\frac{3}{4}$ time. The beat is a quarter note, grouped into threes by bar lines. You emphasize the feeling of three by accenting each 1 beat in keeping with standard $\frac{3}{4}$ meter. Before going on, remember that a dotted note is equal to the value of the note plus one-half the value of the note (one dotted quarter note = one-and-a-half quarter notes). Clearly then, two dotted quarter notes are equal in value to three quarter notes. By playing a series of dotted quarter notes against a quarter note pulse in $\frac{3}{4}$ time, you produce the effect of a two pulse combined with a three pulse. Hemiola is created by a movement from a three pulse, to a relationship of two to three, as shown below.

The same effect may be created by moving in the opposite direction. Here we begin in $\frac{2}{4}$ time. We now have a quarter-note beat that, as defined by the meter, is felt in groups of two. Our definition of a triplet—three notes played in place of two notes of the same value—serves to create hemiola. The top example below shows how we would move from a two pulse to a relationship of three to two by using a quarter note triplet. In the second example, we break the quarter note triplets into two groups of eighth note triplets to get a different perspective on this rhythm. By creating six triplet notes we can more clearly see the relationship of the two pulse (understood as two groups of three), to the three pulse (breaking up the same six notes into three groups of two). The eighth-note triplet is a common subdivision in jazz and hemiola of this type.

Using either of these techniques yields the same ultimate effect of hemiola. By reversing the direction of movement, however, one creates a very different underlying feeling of pulse.

The above examples yield two-line rhythms, but we may also create hemiola as a one-line rhythm that maintains its polyrhythm in relation to the underlying (but not played) beat. The two examples below create identical rhythms, though each has a different basic meter. The first rhythm is in ¾ and the underlying pulse is felt as groups of three. The second rhythm, in ²⁄₄, is felt as groups of two. Both rhythms move back and forth between pulses in two and pulses in three; the difference is in the underlying feeling (which should be maintained by tapping the foot on the quarter note beat). It may be very difficult to execute these rhythms and especially to produce smooth-sounding transitions and even-sounding pulses. If you have access to a drum machine or sequencer, program these rhythms, listen, and clap or play along until it becomes comfortable. You have only really mastered hemiola when you can play these rhythms quite comfortably, feeling either pulse and maintaining either beat in the tapping of your foot.

Another way of arriving at hemiola is through changing time signatures, also called polymeter. In the next example, a ¾ time signature shifts to ⁶⁄₈. Meter defines the ¾ time signature (played in eighth notes) as having a feeling of three groups of two beats each, whereas ⁶⁄₈ time is felt as two groups of three beats each. In the example the rhythm that is clapped (a simple eighth note pulse) remains constant while the beat (tapped by the foot) goes from groups of three in ¾ to groups of two in ⁶⁄₈. The value of the eighth note remains the same, so the pulse that is clapped keeps the same speed throughout. The beat shifts when the signature changes, so that the tapping foot changes from three to a bar to two to a bar. The underlying feeling (meter) is creating a form of hemiola. This may also be difficult to coordinate, so begin by using a very slow tempo.

Further polyrhythmic effects can be created by mixing a variety of rhythms with the use of changing time signatures.

The concept of polymeter suggests an element of African rhythm that has only found limited application in the West: the additive approach. In general, rhythm can be created either by dividing the pulse into varying note lengths or by adding new rhythms without regard to previous note groupings. These techniques may be called "divisive" and "additive," respectively. The two methods represent very different ways of feeling the creation of rhythm, though they may yield rhythms that sound the same. The Western system of meter and time signature is linked with the divisive approach; the underlying pulse is divided up into measures and varying note values. In an additive approach, rhythmic phrases are added together, one after another, to produce a string of rhythm. Polymeter reflects this in its creation of phrases that may or may not contain the same number of beats. The divisive method may offer a nice, consistent system for producing rhythm, but the additive approach may be more natural.

Polyrhythm may extend beyond any of the notions we've described so far. An extreme form of polyrhythm is free rhythm, employing many simultaneous independent rhythmic lines that may lack any vertical coincidence. The pulses and phrases of the lines may not share any common elements of the beat, although they usually maintain separate internal structures in the form of pulse and phrase. Free rhythm of this type has been used in various forms of jazz and by certain twentieth century classical composers. The effect may range from a feeling of suspension, to the cacophonous, to the simply unmusical. The listener's perception, however, is probably conditioned by his or her musical background and experience. What is meaningless noise to one listener may be entirely musical to another.

Drum machines and sequencers give us ready access to all kinds of polyrhythmic effects that would otherwise take years to master, or would be virtually impossible to reproduce.

Experiment with some of the examples here and work out your own extensions of polyrhythm. If you own a drum machine you can do this fairly easily, and the rhythms may suggest some fresh ideas for your own drum parts and song structures.

7
POPULAR RHYTHM TRADITIONS

THE CONVERGENCE OF SEVERAL RHYTHM TRADITIONS has resulted in the diverse array of pop styles that make up today's musical landscape. It will ultimately be to your advantage to know the fine points of rhythm in all these styles, so that you'll be able to apply them intelligently to whatever music you happen to be writing, arranging, producing, or setting to rhythm. Before looking at narrow divisions of rock, funk, country, and jazz, however, it will be helpful to look at the broader categories of music from which they have emerged.

There are two basic traditions which can be seen as "umbrella" styles for all of pop. One of them is the rock tradition, which in its broadest definition can be said to embrace most categories of the popular song. The other is the jazz tradition, which in an equally broad definition might include a large majority of popular instrumental music. Within each of these categories are basic rhythms that can later be expanded and adjusted to fit various spin-off styles. The following discussion will focus on these essential rhythms, presenting them in a two-line format that you can practice using two hands as a preparation for the more complex drum beats that will be presented in Part Three.

As you explore rhythms common to basic popular styles, it's also valuable to begin thinking about ways these rhythms are expanded into complete instrumental arrangements, with specific functions assigned to guitars, keyboards, bass guitars, and supplementary "sweetening" instruments. In this way, rhythm can be seen to encompass much more than drum and percussion parts. You might also start to consider the larger rhythmic issues of form and organization, in which small segments of rhythm are linked together to create songs and complete compositions. Just as we use language, by combining words to form phrases, phrases to make sentences, and sentences to make paragraphs, so do we build extended rhythms from notes to phrases and phrases to sections, with the measure serving to identify the basic structural units.

The influences on pop music have come from an even greater number of sources than we've previously seen. Among the other rhythm traditions that have been absorbed, in varying degrees, into the melting pot of mainstream pop are those of Latin America and the Far East. Though their impact has been limited, these traditions provide the contemporary drummer with extra spice for a well-balanced recipe of rhythm sounds and techniques.

The Rock Tradition. Since the '60s, the term "rock" has come to include a wide range of approaches to popular music. Much of what is also called pop, country, blues, R&B, dance, and even jazz has in recent years been included under the rock heading. There are also many branches of traditional rock, from new wave to heavy metal, with new categories and genres emerging on a regular basis. What is rhythmically fundamental to this popular vocal music is the use of the backbeat.

Some simple backbeat rhythms are shown below. In rock, the most common rhythm consists of eighth notes set in $\frac{4}{4}$ time. The backbeat—or beats 2 and 4—is usually played on the snare drum, with the bass drum hitting beats 1 and 3. Other instruments may be added to provide support on beats 2 and 4.

Dividing backbeat rhythms into two-line rhythms allows us to isolate the backbeat from the bass drum part. Two-line rhythms suggest the use of contrasting pitches and timbres (tone colors) for the upper and lower beats. Though many percussion instruments are of indeterminate pitch, they still can differ in pitch and tone color, as illustrated by the low and high conga drums (tumba and quinta). Indeed, the two-line rhythms shown on the next page are as playable on hand drums, congas, and the piano as they are on a drum set. The examples are labeled as R = right hand (bass drum) and L = left hand (snare drum) because most drummers play the snare with the left hand. If applied to congas or to piano, however, the hands would normally be reversed.

Adding sixteenth notes and letting the backbeat (left) hand participate further in the rhythm yields the "funkier" and freer kinds of beats shown below. These two-pitched rhythms interact to form one rhythm, with the distinguishing backbeat emphasized through accentuation.

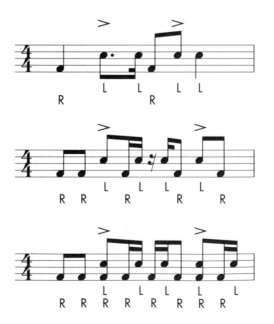

The Full-Band Rhythm Arrangement. A rock band or combo builds on top of rhythms such as these, meaning that each instrument in a band is assigned a part that fits into or supports the basic rhythm stated by the bass drum and snare. The key elements in most bands are drums, bass guitar, one or more "rhythm instruments" (guitars and keyboards are actually chordal, though they serve a vital rhythmic function), and singers. Additional instruments are used as necessary for melodic, harmonic, and rhythmic support. The rhythmic hierarchy starts with the drums and progresses through bass guitar, rhythm instruments, and melody. The drums provide the essential rhythms, including the pulse and backbeat; the bass guitar bridges the drums to the harmony; and the rhythm instruments augment the rhythm and provide harmonic support for the melody. Let's look at the rhythmic role of each instrument.

The bass guitar generally plays linear (single note) parts that are closely related to the drum rhythms but also provide fundamental harmonic information for the other instruments and singers. In many cases the bass guitar plays a simple pulse (usually eighth or quarter notes). If adopting a more rhythmic role it may play the identical rhythm as the bass drum. This might involve covering the bass drum part while adding other rhythms or it could be limited to playing a portion of the bass drum beat. Bass lines are often ostinato parts (repeating, as with a riff). The only real rule of thumb here is that the bass guitar and the bass drum, sharing the low register, will work together rhythmically in some fundamental way. Any of the right-hand rhythms above (representing the bass drum) can be used as bass line rhythms.

The guitars and keyboards (now able to simulate virtually any instrumental sound, thanks to recent technology) are usually the bridge linking the drums and bass to the vocal or melody. These "rhythm" instruments serve two basic functions. The first is to provide rhythmic support and contrast, and the second is to lay down a harmonic foundation. Usually both functions are fulfilled simultaneously by one instrument, though focusing on one or the other of the two tasks suggests some interesting arrangement possibilities.

In adopting a mostly rhythmic role, the instrument is usually played *staccato* (a very short-sounding note or chord) and is rhythmically active. Sixteenth-note rhythms are common to this approach, as is a pronounced attack. Although harmonic information is being presented, it is not making a very strong statement. The sound of the instrument is sometimes so short and played with such attack as to be essentially non-harmonic, producing a percussive sound almost like a scratch. Guitars and many keyboards have very strong percussive capabilities and may be used strictly for rhythm. The use of guitar in funk or disco tunes is a good example of this kind of approach.

The rhythm instrument may also offer harmonic information with very little rhythmic content. These instrumental parts are often called "pads" because they pad the overall sound with chordal harmony. A classic example of a pad is the organ part in the Percy Sledge song "When a Man Loves a Woman." In earlier popular song forms, the harmonic information was most often played on electronic organ or strings. Now these sustained harmonic backdrops can be assigned virtually any sound quality by using a synthesizer or a sampler.

The most common style of rhythm playing on guitar or keyboard manages to combine these two functions, using sharp attack and well-placed sustain to both reinforce the rhythm and provide the harmony. The rhythms are often built from the bass drum and bass guitar parts, offering simple, basic outlines of the more complex drum/bass combination. The harmonic aspect of this approach supports the vocal line by including melody notes, often as the top note of the chord.

Background vocals, horn sections, and other instruments may be used to add further levels of rhythmic and harmonic information. At the top of the rhythmic hierarchy are solo vocal and instrumental melodies (lead vocal, lead guitar, and so on). Melodies tend to have the greatest rhythmic freedom, relying on the other instruments to provide the underlying support.

Rhythmic arranging requires attention to two basic types of organization: vertical and horizontal. Vertical arranging relates to the interaction of all instruments at any given moment. It tells you where the instruments coincide rhythmically, and what the cumulative rhythmic effect is when they don't. The arranger who is focusing on vertical structure is concerned with the placement of the guitar relative to the hi-hat, with using a bass guitar note to fill a space left by the snare, with finding a shaker part that will offer rhythmic counterpoint to the melody. In short, he is concerned with the instrumental groove that will be used throughout the song and that will provide an appropriate backdrop for the vocal.

Horizontal arranging refers to the order and interaction of the sections of a song. It describes the movement from part to part, such as the flow from introduction to verse to chorus, and so on. Horizontal arranging is necessarily defined in rhythmic terms, with the measure serving as the central unit of measurement. Rhythmic ideas tend to be in two- and four-measure phrases, which are developed into song sections that are usually eight, twelve, or sixteen measures long. The exact makeup of a phrase is dependent on the subtle interaction of all musical elements, and rests in part on the perception of the listener. Although phrases in popular songs tend to be very simple, with obvious signposts such as accented down-beats and resolutions to the primary chord, the instrumental phrase can be more mysterious and hard to define. Programming drum machines to create song forms may help you to structure interesting phrases.

The Jazz Tradition. The contemporary instrumental music tradition may be generally placed under the heading of jazz. In this sense jazz could include music also called rock, blues, funk, fusion, new age, and even country (David Grisman's mandolin-based instrumental music, for example, is a rare matching of jazz with bluegrass). At the core of the jazz tradition, however, is a rhythm that is also used widely in the blues: the shuffle or swing beat. It is to this basic concept that we will limit the present discussion, though you should keep in mind that these rhythms are expanded and developed to a great degree in the real world of instrumental music, and also in Part Three of this book.

Shuffle and swing rhythms share a characteristic division of the beat by triplets rather than by straight eighth notes. Triplet rhythms are generally more complex than eighth-note rhythms because they suggest twelve divisions in a standard measure of $\frac{4}{4}$, rather than eight. As in rock, the backbeat is generally played by the snare drum. The basic two-line rhythms shown below are written for two hands, which correspond to typical bass drum and snare drum patterns.

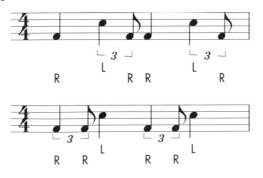

These rhythms are quite simple, employing only the first and third notes within each triplet. The following two-line rhythms suggest triplet ideas that are more developed. The backbeat may or may not be overtly stated, but it is implied in the underlying meter. Notice that the third one of these rhythms include hemiola (a simultaneous subdivision of the beat by two and three). This is a somewhat natural occurrence when using a three-note subdivision because groups of six may be organized as two groups of three, or three groups of two.

Rhythm in the Jazz Band. The rhythmic relationship of instruments in a typical jazz group is not unlike that in a rock band. The hierarchy still progresses from drums to bass, then to rhythm instruments, and finally to melody. The difference is that in a jazz unit the instruments often interact with more freedom and complexity than they might in a song-oriented setting.

While the jazz tradition has expanded in many different directions, two important elements have remained relatively constant. These are syncopation and improvisation, and both have occurred in simple form as well as in relatively complex manifestations. In early jazz groups, including the big bands of the swing era, syncopation was expressed in straightforward, off-the-beat accents by the horn section, in the percussive accompaniment of the piano, and in the single note lines of the soloist. Charlie Christian's guitar solos often made use of plainly stated, easy-to-follow syncopation. Many jazz soloists have played in straight eighth notes while syncopating the interior accents, as in the following:

In later small group approaches, evolving from the bebop groups of the 1940s, the syncopation factor began to be expanded throughout the ensemble, yielding even more complex offbeats that eventually spilled over into polyrhythm.

Improvisation in early jazz was carried out by the soloist, while the back-up musicians provided solid and predictable support. Later groups have turned improvisation into a complex, interactive form, in which each musician creates spontaneously while leading, answering, and always listening to the collaborating players.

In most jazz the complexities of syncopation and improvisation occur within a broad structural framework. This framework may be borrowed directly from a song. In fact, many jazz compositions are arrangements of popular songs, using the original melody and chord structure as a jump-off point for improvisation. The traditional jazz format consists of a statement of the melody (the head), followed by a series of improvisations based on the melody, and ending with a restatement of the melody. Rhythmic frameworks—the horizontal arrangement cited earlier—may take a number of forms, from the twelve-bar blues, to the standard thirty-two bar song form (four eight-bar sections often organized as AABA), to the more contemporary verse/chorus format, to the freer arrangements of current bands.

Within these broad formats, jazz employs several rhythmic concepts that challenge the player and the listener. Among them are additive rhythms that are polyrhythmic and polymetric, yielding contrary lines that may share only the underlying pulse. A loosely enforced pulse may permeate the music, but there is no standard time signature or subdivision of the beat. This approach sometimes extends to free rhythm, where even the underlying pulse is irregular or completely ignored.

Current drum machine technology provides easy access to syncopation, polyrhythm, and polymeter, and can even express subtlety in rhythmic feel. The most notable shortcoming is an inability to improvise. Though AI (artificial intelligence) holds the promise of machine-generated improvisation, and has delivered some "composing" software already, true improvisation is sure to remain a uniquely human capability.

The Latin-American Tradition. The music of Latin America has had a two-sided impact on North-American popular music. On one hand, the Latin Americans were the first in the Western Hemisphere to assimilate African rhythms and were vital in fusing these traditions with Western popular music. On the other hand, the native forms and rhythms of Latin music have had their own profound influence on contemporary American and European sounds. In the 1950s the United States was won over by the popular bossa nova, samba, and cha cha dances. All of these employ the standard feel, or meter, of Western music rather than the backbeat, but they bring it to syncopated embellishments and a battery of percussion instruments, both of which have an African ancestry.

The bossa nova is the most popular and widely performed of these styles. Its underlying pulse emphasizes beats 1 and 3, and lacks any sort of backbeat accentuation. The bass line in its most basic application reflects this metrical structure.

In popular use this bass line has been embellished in various ways, using smaller note values to push more strongly onto the accented 1 and 3 beats.

In conjunction with the meter and the bass line, there is a syncopated, two-measure pattern that epitomizes the bossa nova feel. It's a standard clave rhythm and is used in all forms of Latin music.

Combining the clave rhythm with the bass line to form a two-line rhythm yields the following pattern. It occurs with subtle variations in different bossa novas.

Sometimes the clave rhythm is altered slightly so that it becomes an extended series of dotted quarter notes. This is achieved by stretching the last note in the first measure one eighth note beyond its normal position. Two versions of this rhythm are shown below. The first is written in $\frac{4}{4}$; the second is in $\frac{8}{4}$ and shows the full effect of dotted quarter notes in a connected series.

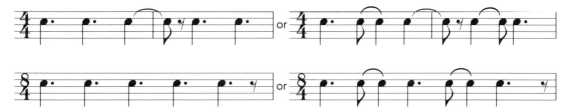

You will remember that the dotted quarter note, when played against a quarter-note pulse, can produce hemiola by imposing a two pulse over three-beat groups. In this case it is done in $\frac{4}{4}$ time, creating five groups of three eighth notes (or five dotted quarter notes). In the lower example, a single eighth rest is required to fill out the measure.

The bossa nova has crept into jazz, providing a welcome alternative to standard swing and setting up a loose, comfortable groove for improvisation. The prominent use of dotted quarter notes, along with bossa bass lines and Latin-American percussion, have added a Latin flavor to numerous instrumentals and popular songs, among them Steely Dan's "Aja" and Janis Ian's "At Seventeen."

Another influential Latin-American form is the samba. It has had a particular impact on American rock and jazz rhythms, and has been noticeably present in the recent music of jazz players like Pat Metheny, Wayne Shorter, and Chick Corea. The reason for this is not hard to understand. There are few rhythms in the world that are as exciting as an uptempo samba played on an array of drums and hand percussion, and it provides an ideal setting for soaring, virtuosic improvisation.

The roots of the samba are undoubtedly African as well as Latin-American. In the classic Brazilian or carnival samba, the central rhythm is a two-measure phrase subdivided into eighth notes. The example below is a two-line rhythm usually played on a two-pitched bell, or sometimes on two different-sized conga drums.

As integrated into American use, this rhythm would be more accurately written in cut-time, or as the sixteenth-note rhythm in $\frac{4}{4}$ shown below.

In either case the samba has a consistent pattern of tension and resolution. The beginning of the rhythm is stable, played on the beat or on simple divisions of it; the middle of the rhythm is unstable, with offbeats creating a very brief polyrhythm; the end of the rhythm returns to the stability of the beat. Thus we enter and exit the rhythm playing in a stable, pulse-oriented manner, with the interior of the rhythm providing tension. The following examples share this basic characteristic.

Some other popular Latin-American rhythms are shown in the following examples. You may recognize a few of them from their occasional use in pop music, although it's difficult to trace the exact impact of these approaches on current commercial styles. Note that some of these are two-line rhythms and some are three-line rhythms, all indicating multiple drum pitches. An x is used to indicate a rim sound.

Eastern Traditions. The ongoing interaction of world cultures, made possible by travel, trade, and communications technology, has brought about a fruitful exchange of musical ideas and has yielded some intriguing hybrid forms. Popular music is a veritable melting pot of musical and rhythmic influences, blending European harmony with African rhythm, and incorporating other elements along the way. The music of the Far East has been part of this mixture, contributing unique approaches to timbre, rhythm, and form. Indonesian music has had an interesting, though limited, impact. The gamelan music of Java and Bali, with its interlocking rhythms and a range of drums and metallophones, has influenced a number of Western composers working in the jazz and classical idioms. Other Eastern traditions have been absorbed and incorporated into Western approaches in varying degrees, but none have had quite the exposure and impact of the music of India, with its highly developed concept of rhythm and complex system of scales and improvisation.

Indian music often employs drums with specific pitch and melodic responsibilities. The primary drum, the tabla, is a hand drum in which pitches are generated through very involved hand and finger muting and stretching of the drum head. The Indian word for rhythm is *tāla*, which also refers to specific rhythm patterns that combine to form compositions. The northern and southern Indian traditions are somewhat different, though they also share certain elements. In general, northern tālas are polymetric, stringing rhythms together in an additive fashion. Southern tālas are organized into groups of three and four, called *jātis*, and may be slightly more divisive in concept. A common northern tāla, called *tintal*, strings together four groups of four beats to form a regular pattern of rhythm. A common southern tāla uses regular groupings of 4 + 2 + 2. Other tālas, however, are built on more complex, irregular groups of five and seven. These musical structures, commonly called odd time signatures or "odd times," have found their way into both progressive jazz and classical traditions (think of Dave Brubeck's "Take Five"), and have even turned up in popular song forms, such as the measures of $\frac{7}{4}$ in the Beatles' "All You Need Is Love." It seems possible that odd times will play an increasingly active role in popular music as listeners become more acquainted with the sound of these rhythms.

Other elements of Indian music have been employed by jazz, pop, and classical musicians. Free rhythm has been used as a compositional device to provide an introduction or "invocation" to a piece of music, as in the Freddie Hubbard tune "Red Clay," or even in the beginning of the Bruce Hornsby track "Look Out Any Window." Indian melodic and harmonic approaches have turned up in the music of the Beatles, John McLaughlin, and John Coltrane. It is likely that Far Eastern ideas will continue to influence American music, and vice versa, as the world's music continues to become more accessible to all of its inhabitants.

PART THREE

DRUM
BEATS
IN POPULAR
MUSIC

8
A GUIDE
TO USE

FROM THE BASICS OF RHYTHM AND PERCUSSION, we now turn to specific beats as they are
used in various styles of popular music. For the most part, these are simple
models that may be modified and adapted to particular songs, and played
on traditional percussion instruments or current electronic machinery.

Contemporary drum beats reflect a wide diversity of influences in Western popular music. But what ties all these different threads together is the
overriding force of the ever-present backbeat. With the exception of Latin-
American forms, the African-derived backbeat dominates the rhythmic
structure of all popular styles, from rock and roll to funk, blues, and
country. It's what gives the beats their tension and locks together the
groove. And it will be the starting point for most of the rhythmic patterns
covered in this section.

In looking at drum beats used for different pop styles, you'll really be
tracing the evolution of the backbeat through varying degrees of complexity. For this reason, it is a good idea to follow an orderly progression
through the section, rather than skip around from chapter to chapter.
While it's important to know the special characteristics of individual styles,
the fact is that many of these beats are equally at home in a number of
different musical settings. By looking at the underlying structure of beats,
rather than simply plugging beats into stylistic slots, you'll develop a much
more flexible approach to drumming and rhythm playing.

In this section you'll begin by outlining a basic backbeat pattern as it is
played on the drum set, divided among the bass drum, snare, and ride

patterns. You'll then take this formula through its application to rock and pop drum beats. As the patterns get more complex, they move into the sophisticated rhythms of R&B and funk. By changing the subdivision of the beat, while retaining the essential backbeat approach, you'll find yourself in the domain of blues and jazz. Further rhythmic variations yield approaches common to country music and the innovative, relatively new reggae. The final style in this section, Latin, is the only one of these forms that does not use the backbeat in its traditional rhythms, although it's quite possible to play patterns that combine a Latin feel within the backbeat. Concluding this section are discussions of fills and embellishments, which make use of additional instruments often used with drum set parts and often found on drum machines.

As you progress through these various types and styles of beats, you'll begin to form a larger picture of the way drum beats are constructed; ultimately you'll be able to identify almost any drum beat as a variation or combination of the rhythms shown in these examples. Here you'll begin to gain insight into the overall theory and organization of drumming, beyond just picking up specific beats; you'll approach the goal of thinking like a drummer.

Notating the Drum Set. Drum set beats use a very simple system of notation. A standard music stave is used, with different spaces representing different parts of the drum set. Most of the rhythms that you will be looking at will include only a ride pattern (usually played on the closed hi-hat or ride cymbal and written with x's rather than regular note heads), a snare drum rhythm, and a kick (bass) drum rhythm. (For the sake of clarity, and true to contemporary recording studio practice, we refer to the bass drum as the kick drum, or simply as the kick, to distinguish it from other bass instruments such as bass guitar.) A simple rhythm showing the spaces in the stave used for the ride, snare, and kick is shown below:

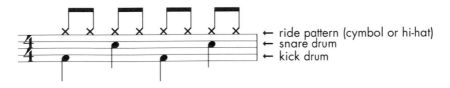

In later examples other instruments will be introduced, all of which were first discussed in Chapter Four. They are notated as follows:

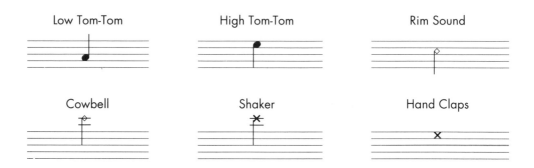

As you begin to read the examples in the following chapters, remember that the position of the notes on the page will help you decide when they are played. For example, two notes that are directly above and below each other sound on the same beat; a note that appears halfway between two notes is played halfway in time between the two notes.

Accenting is indicated by the symbol >. If your drum machine is capable of more than two levels of accenting you should experiment with this. As discussed earlier, variations in accenting will help you achieve a more flexible and loose feel on the machine.

More Tips on Using This Section. As you progress through the examples, you will find that the essence of most drum beats boils down to a simple two-line rhythm carried on the kick and snare drums. This basic rhythm has its roots in more primitive instruments that were played with two hands, usually on a single instrument with two relative pitches (i.e., logs, bells, drums, and so on). One hand played a lower pitch and one a higher. In these examples you will also note that the ride pattern has something of an independent function, usually maintaining the pulse.

Many of these examples are expressed in one-, two-, and four-measure patterns. These lengths tend to be the best building blocks for composing drum parts. As you grow more comfortable with these beats, and with rhythm work in general, you should begin to create your own beats that are similar to the patterns shown in any given category. One way to do this is to extract single measures from some of the longer patterns, and then recombine them in new ways.

If you play an instrument other than drums, you'll find that an awareness of the beats in this section will help out when you're working with a drummer or programming a drum machine. You might also try playing some of these rhythms on your own instrument. From two-note rhythms to chordal rhythm parts, there are numerous ways to interpret drum set rhythms on any instrument. Players who are involved with drum machines will probably want to use many of these beat patterns as they begin to program different rhythm ideas for their music.

But whatever your involvement in rhythm, keep experimenting and trying different things. And remember: there's a good reason why musical activity is called "playing." Enjoy it.

9
ROCK
AND
POP

CURRENT ROCK AND POP MUSIC, as discussed earlier, really encompasses a broad spectrum of approaches. While the dynamics and timbre of rhythm tracks may differ depending on the style—powerful and full-bodied for hard rock; somewhat more restrained and colorful for melodic pop—the underlying beat patterns are quite similar.

We have already set the stage for the following examples by establishing the importance of the backbeat in popular music and by tracing the evolution of the modern drum set. At this point you have a clear understanding of the backbeat and are familiar with the basic parts of a set of drums. Now we'll look at the way those two essential elements combine to form relatively simple patterns used in rock music.

The Backbeat on the Drum Set. The example below shows a basic backbeat as played on the drum set. Two critical functions are accomplished in this simple example. The top line, or ride pattern (played most commonly on the closed hi-hat), sets up the eighth-note pulse. The kick drum and the snare drum form a two-line rhythm that presents the backbeat in its simplest form.

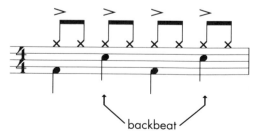

In this example the two-line rhythm formed by kick and snare drums is actually a simple quarter-note pulse—the primary beats. You will remember from our discussions of meter and the backbeat that the backbeat sets up a kind of call and response relationship. This is created by answering the kick drum (beats 1 and 3) with the snare drum (beats 2 and 4). The backbeat answers back, providing the meter with a kind of built-in tension. Although the kick/snare rhythm is a simple pulse, the contrast between the two sounds—the big bass boom of the kick drum and the sharp crack of the snare drum—underscores a distinct metric feel, evolved from two-handed rhythms.

The simplest extension of the backbeat model adds rhythmic interest by adding to the kick drum pattern, as seen in the examples below. These drum beats maintain all of the elements in our original model: the eighth-note pulse in the ride pattern, the kick on the 1 and 3, and the backbeat, or beats 2 and 4, on the snare drum. But they develop the two-line rhythm created by the kick/snare pattern beyond the basic quarter-note pulse. Starting with our original backbeat model, we begin thinking about the space between each kick and snare beat (each quarter note of the measure). Our ride-pattern pulse fills in each space with an additional eighth note beat, called the "and" beat. Each of these "and" beats provide a place for an additional kick drum beat. In one measure of $\frac{4}{4}$ time there are four of these "and" beats, called the "and of one" following the 1 beat, the "and of 2," the "and of 3," and the "and of 4." Each of these "and" beats may have a kick drum beat or not. Remember that these beats still include the kick drum on the 1 and 3 beats and the snare on the 2 and 4, so that the quarter-note pulse remains a part of the two-line snare/kick rhythm.

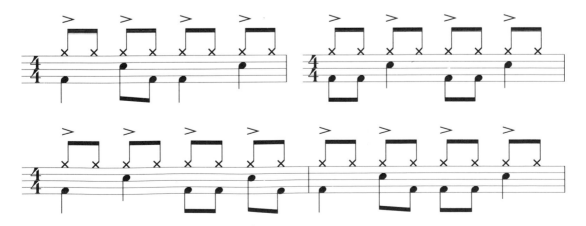

Using these "and" beat options for the kick drum enables you to create many of the basic drum beats found in a large number of contemporary songs. You might recognize the second example above as the beat played by Ringo in the introduction to (and throughout most of) the Beatles song "Sgt. Pepper's Lonely Hearts Club Band." Literally thousands of songs use this basic drum beat—or similar ones—through the majority of the song, or in particular sections.

Remember that accenting is indicated by the mark shown above the ride pattern. The primary beats carry an accent, while the "and" beats are unaccented. The accent applies to the kick and the snare beats as well as the ride pattern. The use of accenting is very important in establishing the appropriate feel in these rhythms.

Developing the Snare Drum. As seen in the next example, you may also use the "and" counts for additional snare beats. Here proper accenting is crucial in bringing out the backbeats. While used quite frequently, these patterns are less common than the simple kick drum rhythms already developed. This is probably because, even with proper accenting, any additional snare beats can draw away from the simple backbeat feel.

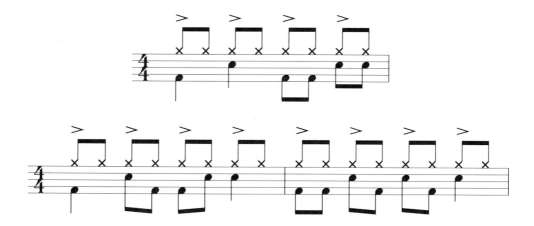

Adding Syncopation. There are other ways to expand the basic backbeat. In the previous examples, you maintained either kick or snare statements on all four of the primary beats. In the next example, you'll eliminate the kick drum from beat 3. This creates a syncopation because beat 3, which is one of the primary beats, is no longer played in the two-line rhythm created by the kick/snare pattern.

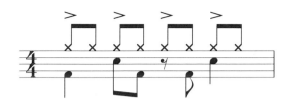

This is the most common type of primary beat syncopation for the following reason. The 1 beat is the most important beat (and center of both rhythmic arrival and departure), and beats 2 and 4 are created the backbeat. Thus the 3 beat is the least important of the four primary ones. It serves as a secondary 1 beat and helps to distinguish the four-beat cycle (quadruple meter) from the two-beat cycle (duple meter). By not playing the kick at this point you emphasize the importance of the 1 beat and thus give additional importance to the cycle of four, as you now must return to the 1 beat to resolve the cycle.

This rhythm has a syncopated sound and feel even though the ride pattern plays a continuous pulse that includes every primary beat. The pulse-keeping function of the ride pattern should be thought of separately from the two-line rhythm created by the kick/snare pattern.

Other patterns use different approaches to the three-beat syncopation. Note that both the kick and the snare drum parts are developed below, though rhythmic interest is provided mostly by the kick drum. The two-measure rhythm uses the 3 beat syncopation only in the second measure. A typical use of this type of beat might be as a pattern in the verse of a song, with the chorus releasing to one of the more basic beats, as in the Rolling Stones classic "Honky-Tonk Woman."

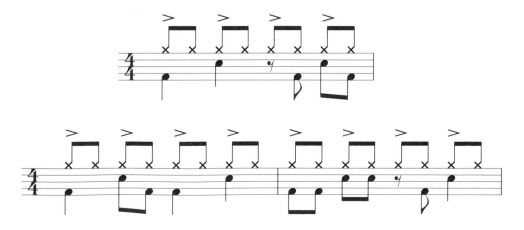

Altering the Ride Pattern. The pulse-keeping function of the ride pattern may be altered from the standard eighth-note pulse you have used up until now. While the eighth-note pulse is most common, other divisions of the pulse may also be used. In the example below, the ride pattern is reduced to quarter notes, sounding only on the primary beats. Meanwhile, the kick and snare rhythm is a version of one of our earlier patterns. This ride pattern is most appropriate for faster tempos and/or within sparser arrangements. As with all ride patterns, they are most commonly played on the closed hi-hat, though they may also be played on the ride cymbal. Occasionally other instruments such as cowbell, woodblock, or even tom-tom may substitute here in place of cymbals.

The next examples demonstrate ride patterns appropriate to slower and faster tempos, using kick and snare beats familiar from previous examples. The double-time ride pattern is common in slower tempos and ballads. With the use of sixteen notes per measure, the accenting function becomes increasingly important in maintaining the sense of the primary beats—the quarter-note pulse. If you are playing this beat on the drums, or if three levels of accenting are available on your drum machine or sequencers, try putting the strongest accent on the primary beats, a secondary accent on the "and" beats, and an unaccented note on the intermediary sixteenth notes (the "e" and "a" beats).

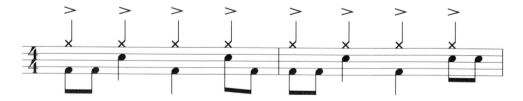

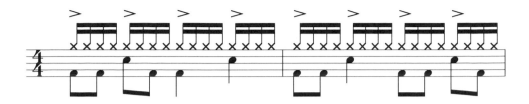

How Does Rock Rhythm Differ from Pop? So far we've discussed rock and pop as one category, without distinguishing between the two. The fact is that, in terms of rhythm structure, the drum beats you have looked at here would be as likely to appear in one style as in the other, the two being very closely related. The differences between rock and pop can be heard more in the way the drums sound on a finished recording than in the patterns actually played. In rock the drums are likely to be featured more, mixed louder in relation to the other instruments and voice, than they are on a pop record. Rock drums are usually played more forcefully, and there will usually be more fills than in a normal pop drum arrangement. But a basic backbeat approach and simple rhythms are equally common to both styles.

Keep in mind that these types of basic, backbeat-oriented beats may be used in virtually every style of contemporary music, though perhaps less frequently than in rock and pop styles.

10
R&B
AND
FUNK

AMONG THE BRANCHES OF CONTEMPORARY "hit" music, rhythm and blues (R&B) and funk offer particularly exciting possibilities for rhythmic development. From James Brown to Grandmaster Flash to Run-DMC, the rhythm has always been a prominent feature of this sound, and has been the testing ground for innovations in structure, instrumental technique, and electronics.

By further developing the backbeat rhythms that were introduced in the previous chapter, we can create rhythms that are common to the sounds of R&B and funk. Again there is a lot of overlapping of rhythms in contemporary music, and, as important as it is to recognize differences in style, it is equally important to follow the evolution of rhythms and see how they are related. Notice that you can simplify these drum beats just a bit and they become the same beats discussed in the previous chapter. And though the rhythms are more complex, the backbeat remains prominent.

Developing the Kick Drum—Sixteenth Notes. You have already seen that the kick drum provides most of the rhythmic interest in common drum set patterns. Here we take this further by introducing a sixteenth-note subdivision of the beat.

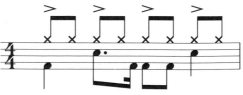

Notice that the kick-drum beats no longer necessarily correspond to all the pulse beats in the eighth-note ride pattern. In the example we have added the sixteenth note prior to beat 3 (the "a" of beat 2) to our basic backbeat rhythm. In this case the sixteenth note is a simple push beat on to beat 3, more of an embellishment than a syncopation. The most common rhythmic use of sixteenth notes is as embellishment beats, usually pushing on to either the kick or the snare, on one or more of the primary beats.

Opening up the drum rhythm to sixteenth notes can be important to the drummer's ability to support other instruments and to create fills and embellishments. This particular drum beat could serve in either a simple or complex musical environment.

The next examples elaborate on the use of the sixteenth note in the kick drum part, primarily as an embellishment beat. Again it is useful to think of these beats without the additional sixteenth notes and see how they have been developed from the basic rhythms you saw in the previous chapter.

When you use more complex rhythms such as these you'll want to pay particular attention to accenting. The additional sixteenth notes are usually played more quietly, which is appropriate for an embellishment. The primary beats will carry the primary accents, the "and" beats will be played more quietly, and the "e" and "a" beats more quietly still.

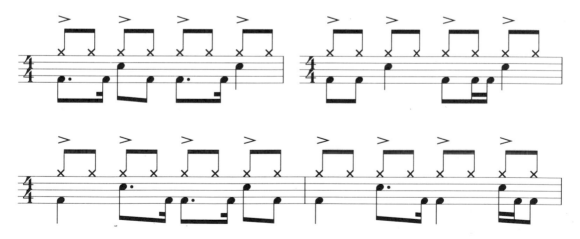

The following shows a sixteenth-note kick drum beat used independent of a primary beat. As in our initial example, you play the "a" of 2, but this time the kick does not play the following 3 beat. This kind of use creates a syncopated-feeling rhythm. It either feels as if the sixteenth-note is left hanging, or as if the 3 beat has been "anticipated" (played early).

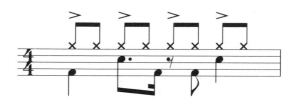

Drum beats such as this are common in the broad style often called funk. Funk can include both progressive pop and jazz styles. In recent years it has also been characterized by the "slap" bass guitar sound, which, through a special right-hand "slapping" technique, produces a twangy, popping sound that interacts closely with the drums. Note that the type of funky syncopation in the rhythm above is most likely to take place around the 3 beat, just as you saw in our initial rock syncopation. Again this is because the 3 beat is the least important of the four primary beats.

Next are more examples of syncopated sixteenth-note subdivisions within the backbeat context. Care must be taken in using these rhythms because they will tend to dominate a musical situation. They leave little room for other rhythmic ideas or counterpoint.

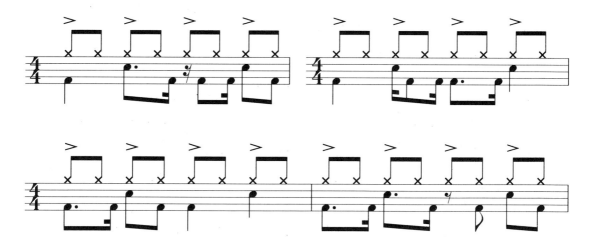

Developing the Snare—Sixteenth Notes and Substitute Backbeats. You can use sixteenth notes with the snare drum just as you did with the kick drum. The snare continues to provide the accented backbeat, with the embellishment beats commonly unaccented.

Snare-drum embellishments are especially good for adding to a feeling of rhythmic motion. Often snare embellishments such as these are really very short fills that connect larger song sections. As in the previous kick drum examples, these additional snare beats occasionally fall between pulse beats in the ride pattern.

Here are some snare examples that actually pull the snare off of one of the two backbeats. The first example, similar to what Ringo Starr used in the Beatles' "Tomorrow Never Knows," shows an accented snare beat on the "and" of 3, with no snare on the 4 beat. You might call this a "substitute backbeat" because this "and of 3" beat is fulfilling the normal backbeat function, though not in the normal location. Notice how all of these examples may be understood as substituting for the backbeat rather than simply omitting it.

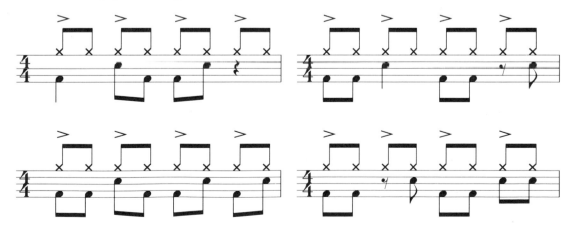

It is more common to substitute for the 4 beat than the 2 beat because the change occurs later in the measure and is less disruptive to the overall rhythm. In certain cases, substitutions may be on either the "and" beats or on the sixteenth note "e" and "a" beats. The concept of "substitute back-beat" provides a means of creating highly syncopated rhythms that retain the basic form of the contemporary backbeat pattern.

Kick/Snare Conversations. The interaction between the snare drum and the kick drum provides the primary focus in all of the drum set rhythms examined so far. The following examples combine the use of sixteenth-note subdivisions in both the kick and the snare, creating an even more pronounced interaction between the two. The ride pattern retains the simple accented eighth-note pulse.

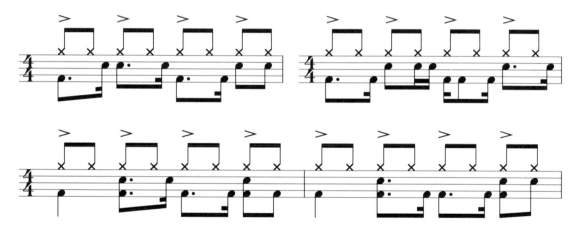

There are only two levels of accenting indicated in these examples, though busy beats such as these would benefit from more subtle degrees of accentuation. If you are playing these beats, or programming them into a drum machine or sequencer that will allow several levels of accenting, you should experiment with subtle shifts of volume throughout the beat. Generally you will want to use a diminishing volume scale, moving from louder to softer from the primary beats to the "and" beats to the "e" and "a" beats.

By thinking of these and most all drum patterns as kick/snare conversations, you gain insight into the way a drummer usually expresses the natural feeling of playing a drum set. It encourages you to think of the drum set as a single instrument, rather than as a group of distinct sounds.

Developing the Ride Pattern. Any of the examples discussed so far could use different pulse rates for the ride patterns, such as in the examples below. Quarter-note ride patterns will work, but sixteenth-note rides would be much more common in these contexts, coinciding with sixteenth-note subdivisions in the kick and snare.

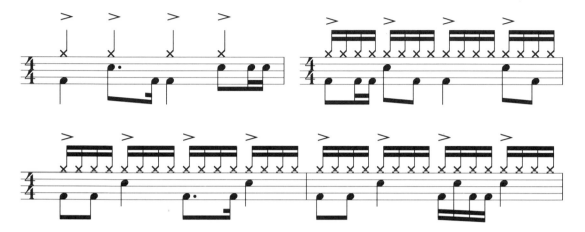

In the next example, we have provided a simple and familiar kick/snare pattern while breaking up the straight pulse-keeping function of the ride. Here the ride rhythm is adjusted so that all the notes in the eighth-note pulse are still played, yet the "and" beats are divided into two sixteenth notes. The resulting three-note combinations (not to be confused with triplets) maintain a strong sense of beat and provide increased movement.

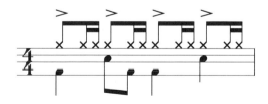

Note that the three-note combinations push from the "and" beats on to the primary beats, emphasizing the quarter-note pulse. This is especially useful in faster tempos that still call for a double-time feeling. The Stevie Wonder hit "Superstitious" employs this kind of ride pattern (played, as is typical, on the closed hi-hat). Three-note combinations working in the other direction (from the primary pulse to an "and" beat) would not provide as strong or propulsive a rhythm.

In the examples below, the ride is shown playing a more independent and less pulse-oriented rhythm. This expands the beat into a three-line rhythm since the ride pattern is interacting with the kick/snare pattern as an equal or even more developed part of the overall sound. These types of drum beats are heard most often in fusion and other jazz-tinged styles as well as in certain Latin-influenced approaches.

By using this three-line approach to drumming, you can begin to see how some very complex rhythms can be developed. The key to making them work is to listen to the combined effect of the three lines as well as to each independent part. They've got to work together in an organic way. When playing complicated ride patterns it is advisable to keep the kick and snare parts simple. That way you'll avoid an overly busy drum part that diverts attention from the music as a whole (unless you're playing a drum solo that is looking for attention).

11
BLUES
AND
JAZZ

IN ALL THE PREVIOUS DRUM BEAT EXAMPLES, reflecting basic approaches to playing rock and funk, we have divided our primary quarter-note beat in twos (eighth-notes) and fours (sixteenth notes). Blues and jazz employ shuffle and swing rhythms, in which the primary beats are divided into threes (triplets). Shuffle and swing beats also bring up the important question of "feel," which will ultimately have an impact on your approach to programming a drum machine. For now, let's take a look at some of the standard patterns used in this music.

The Shuffle. The basic shuffle beat is expressed in the ride pattern in the example below. The first and third notes in each triplet (the downbeat and "ta" beat) are sounded to create the shuffle feel. This is almost like playing straight eighth notes except with a lazier approach to the "and" beat so that it occurs later in time, becoming a triplet "ta" beat rather than an "and" beat. In this example the kick and snare play the most basic backbeat pattern. As in previous examples, the downbeat is accented and the inter-mediary notes are unaccented.

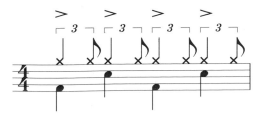

Apart from being used in the blues, the shuffle beat has been applied to rock and has provided a powerful, rolling, forward momentum to many songs in that style. Bruce Springsteen used it successfully in "Kitty's Back," as did Billy Ocean in his number one hit, "When the Going Gets Tough (The Tough Get Going)." Tears for Fears also applied it to their number one song, "Everybody Wants to Rule the World."

Since the shuffle rhythm is an adaptation, almost a lazy man's version of a straight eighth-note pulse, it's easy to adapt any of the all-eighth-note ride examples from the basic backbeat rhythm to shuffle beats, such as those in the examples below. The backbeat feel remains intact.

The ⁶⁄₈ Blues Rhythm. A slow version of the shuffle beat, with all the triplets in the ride filled in, is usually written in ⁶⁄₈ as shown next. This approach has become something of a style in itself, sometimes referred to as "slow blues," and is used in such classic tunes as "Stormy Monday" and "Spoonful." The ⁶⁄₈ time signature has two groups of three eighth notes in each measure. Although not written as triplets, the effect is an even more pronounced feeling of groups of three than in the basic shuffle. The kick and snare drums provide rhythms very similar to the shuffle beat within this framework, only slower. The snare drum still provides a backbeat (the 4 beat in ⁶⁄₈), despite the time signature.

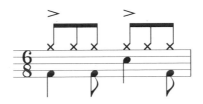

Below are shown additional versions of $\frac{6}{8}$ beats. Note that in the first example we have created kick and snare sixteenth-note embellishments in a few places. In the second example, the ride pattern is subdivided into sixteenth-note triplets. When done simply, in a slow tempo, this very small subdivision may sound quite smooth and comfortable. We will look a bit more into this kind of sixteenth-note triplet subdivision in the final section of this chapter.

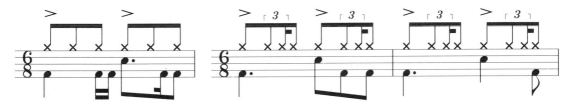

The Swing Beat. The basic rhythm of traditional jazz is called "swing." The format is the same as the shuffle beat, though the basic ride rhythm is slightly more sparse. In swing, the "ta" beat is only played prior to the 1 and 3 beats. This makes the ride rhythm closer to a simple quarter-note pulse, creating a less defined and more spacious environment than the shuffle pattern. Here the kick and snare are creating the basic backbeat rhythm, appropriate to dance-oriented forms of jazz prevalent in the 1930s (such as played by Benny Goodman and Tommy Dorsey). Steady rhythms such as this one tended to reinforce the pulse created by the traditional "walking" melody played on string bass.

As jazz developed, the snare became used more for embellishment, though the sense of backbeat was generally maintained. In the examples below the kick and snare are syncopated, and both jobs of pulse keeping and backbeat accenting are maintained by the ride pattern. The 2 and 4 beats in the ride pattern carry a stronger accent than the 1 or 3 beats, with the intermediary triplets remaining unaccented. Note the frequent use of the "ta" beats played on kick and snare. These beats anticipate the downbeat, providing a quirky rhythmic feel; they often coincide with accents played on rhythm instruments such as guitar or piano.

Syncopation is often referred to as the hallmark of jazz, and within that context has reached new peaks of complexity. Jazz drummers have applied complex syncopations in both written and improvised situations. Among the best known "mainstream" jazz innovators are Max Roach, Elvin Jones, and Buddy Rich.

Developing Swing and the Shuffle. We might call the next example a bass/snare conversation in swing rhythm. Here the kick/snare parts complete some of the triplets, including the second or "ti" notes. In the form shown, the kick plays the primary beat while the snare fills in the middle "ti" and "ta" beats.

The following examples show the use of a triplet or shuffle subdivision on the sixteenth-note level, requiring sixteenth-note triplets (as we saw in one of the $\frac{6}{8}$ blues beats). Here the triplets are used within the context of a backbeat and an eighth-note ride. These triplets may occur in the kick, snare, or ride patterns, or in combinations of any of the three. The basic conventions of accenting, maintenance of the backbeat, and orientation toward kick/snare conversations apply to these patterns as they did to earlier beats.

These rhythms have been used in many styles of pop music. Groups such as the Band in rock and the Crusaders in jazz have reached large audiences with material that employs this approach.

12

COUNTRY, REGGAE, AND LATIN

THE TREMENDOUS CROSS-FERTILIZATION of popular music's various styles makes it difficult to generalize too much about rhythmic convention. In fact it is more and more difficult to pigeonhole a song or composition according to one style.

The Band's tune "Up on Cripple Creek" is an example of a song that is basically country in orientation (indicated mostly by the lyrics), though its underpinning has much in common with the syncopated, fractured sound of funk. The result of this style-mixing is that today, basic rhythm patterns can be used in different forms of music. In this chapter we'll look at three distinctive styles.

Country music is an idiom that has both exerted tremendous influence on, and in turn been greatly influenced by, rock and pop styles. The drum set rhythms outlined in the rock and pop section are almost as common in today's country and folk music. In this section we will look at a particular kind of traditional country music beat: the two-beat rhythm, generally written in what is called "cut-time."

Reggae, a fairly recent addition to U.S. radio airwaves, is one of the more distinctive strains of pop music. At the root of reggae's uniqueness is its rhythmic structure as played on a drum set. Bob Marley's work exemplifies the classic reggae tradition, while the Police, in much of their music, managed to blend reggae rhythms into a more traditional pop song structure. Reggae's intriguing hybrid of backbeat and two-beat rhythms is examined in this section.

Traditional Latin styles have enjoyed great popularity and influence in American pop music since the '50s, with the modern bossa-nova and samba dances attracting particular attention. Among the interesting aspects of these dances is that they do not use the backbeat as a rhythmic device. The rhythms, in fact, are felt on the 1 and 3 beats, just as in the Western classical tradition.

Country. One of the more common rhythmic structures used in country music is called cut-time. On a page of music, cut-time (or *alla breve* in classical music) looks identical to $\frac{4}{4}$ time except that the time signature is given a ¢. In cut-time we feel the beat on the 1 and 3 beats of a four-beat bar rather than on all four primary beats. The rhythm is basically felt in $\frac{2}{2}$ (two half-note beats to the bar), but it is counted in $\frac{4}{4}$. It differs from $\frac{2}{4}$ in that we want to consider all four quarter notes as beats, but we only want to feel two of them. The traditional cut-time carries the backbeat on the 2 and 4 beats though they are not as prominent as in rock and pop. The traditional foot stomp followed by the hand clap indicates the appropriate feel of a two-beat, cut-time rhythm (also called an "oom-pah" beat). A quickness of the tempo is important in establishing the snappy two-beat feeling.

Below you see the same two-beat rhythm using a shuffle or triplet division of the beat rather than the straight eighth notes we saw in the first example. In both examples notice that the ride pattern is not a strict pulse but uses an embellishment beat to move the rhythm on to beat 3 and then back to beat 1.

Next are some simple variations on the basic two-beat approach. The drum set accompaniment in country music is generally very simple, in keeping with the straightforward lyric and melodic approach.

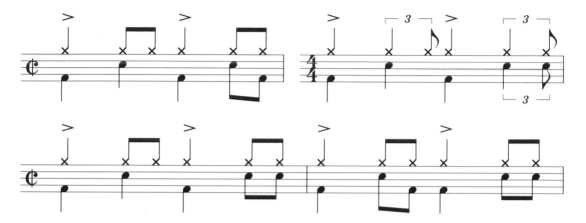

Reggae. Reggae, largely a Jamaican distillation of American rhythm and blues, has a distinctive approach to rhythm characterized by shifting accents and surprising spaces where one would normally expect a sound or a beat. The following example illustrates the essence of the most exciting of the reggae rhythmic innovations on the drum set. The kick/snare pattern is the most basic of backbeats, and the ride pattern is a simple quarter-note pulse. The difference, however, is that the ride pattern has been displaced one eighth note so that the quarter-note pulse is played on the "and" beats rather than on the primary beats.

We could think of this rhythm as two bars of cut-time, with the ride pattern forming an answer beat against the pulse of the kick and snare. The subtle two-beat jumpiness, overlaid on a basic backbeat structure, creates an exciting new rhythm that not only is characteristic of reggae, but has also been used in virtually every other style of popular music in the last decade.

Another reggae innovation, though less original than the last, is shown below. Here the drums omit the 1 beat—the central beat of the bar. This omission is not quite as drastic as it may sound when listened to alone, because in a band setting the bass guitar part will usually still land very strongly on beat 1. Without the normal reinforcement of the kick drum, this provides an unusual feeling of lightness and suspension.

Next, the basic reggae approach is developed to include a double-time feel in addition to the overlaid backbeat and two-beat rhythms. The sixteenth-note pattern in the ride maintains the two-beat jump while introducing a sixteenth-note subdivision. The kick and snare patterns may include sixteenth-note embellishment beats. Reggae rhythms of this kind can become a blanket of interwoven accents, combining various feels with implied beats and overlapping pulses.

Latin—Bossa Nova. The traditional Latin dance form, the bossa nova, came to prominence in the U.S. in the early '60s with the Stan Getz-Astrud Gilberto collaboration ("The Girl from Ipanema"), further entered the popular consciousness through the songs of Antonio Carlos Jobim, and today is an essential rhythmic component of jazz and the occasional rock song. It has come to be commonly interpreted on the drum set as a two-bar rhythm as illustrated on the next page. The diamond-shaped notes indicate the rim sound—a sound created by placing the tip of the drum stick against the snare drum head and hitting the back end of the stick against the rim of the drum. This technique, called cross-sticking, creates a clicking effect similar to the traditional hardwood sound of claves. The rhythm in this example has the claves part used in much traditional Latin-American music. This trademark syncopation is distinguished by its prominent use of the dotted quarter note (a quarter note plus an eighth note in duration).

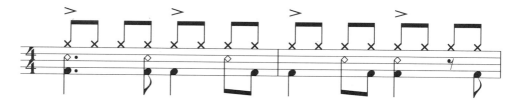

The bossa nova rhythm does not employ the backbeat. The underlying accents are felt only on beats 1 and 3. In the standard kick-drum pattern shown, the "and" beats preceding beats 1 and 3 provide movement on to the accented primary beats.

In the next examples, a new drum is introduced: the tom-tom (hi-tom). It is shown in the top space of the staff. These examples represent two variations of the bossa nova rhythm. The first example is the same as the previous one, except that it reverses the rim or claves rhythm, placing the second measure first. This is a common variation on the traditional form. In the second example, the rhythm is embellished with tom-tom accents. Every rim beat is answered by the hi-tom on the following eighth note. The very end of the rhythm has also been altered, increasing the use of dotted quarter note equivalents. The tom-tom rhythm provides a kind of echo or shadow effect. Experiment with the dotted quarter notes in the clave rhythm when creating other bossa-nova-type rhythms. Notice that kick drum accents are used here, shown in the space just above the kick drum note. Also bear in mind that the hi-tom would be played with the left hand (an obvious point when you note that the right-hand ride pattern is maintained throughout these rhythms).

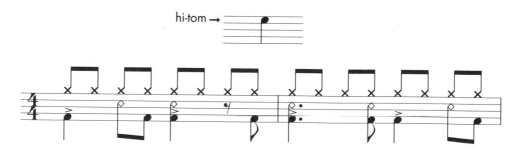

Latin—Samba. The samba, an uptempo, exciting Latin-American dance form, traveled from Brazil to the U.S. via popular musicians like Baden Powell, Milton Nascimento, Airto Moreira, and Gilberto Gil. It has been used extensively in jazz, especially in the flashier, colorful fusion branches of the music.

The pattern below shows the modern drum set interpretation of the traditional samba rhythm. It includes the addition of a low tom-tom (low-tom), which is shown on the second space of the staff, between the kick and the snare. The samba is written and felt in cut-time, as were the traditional country rhythms explored earlier. With the samba, however, there is no backbeat and there is a much higher degree of syncopation. The samba phrase is also a two-bar rhythm. The feeling of the beat could be accurately represented by condensing one of these two-measure patterns into a one-measure pattern that is subdivided by sixteenth notes rather than eighths. In keeping with the cut-time approach, the traditional samba tempo is quick. If you play or program this rhythm at a slow tempo and gradually increase the tempo rate, you can feel the rhythm gradually change from a cumbersome four-beat feel into the light and proper two-beat feel of cut-time.

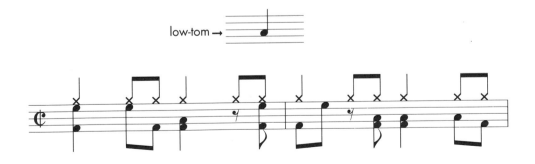

Next, the high- and low-tom patterns are altered for rhythmic interest. Note that the kick and ride patterns remain constant.

An interesting tendency in this kind of tom-tom rhythm (often heard in syncopated two-bar rhythms and discussed in Chapter Seven) is that the first few beats of the first measure and the last few beats of the second measure tend to be more stable parts of the rhythm. The middle part, on the other hand, including the end of measure 1 and the beginning of measure 2, tends to be the place for most of the syncopation. You can think of the overall rhythm as starting and ending with stability on the primary beats, with the tension created by syncopation sandwiched in between. The process of instability leading to stability, or tension to resolution, is an essential source of motion in music and rhythm. It is helpful to keep it in mind when analyzing or composing rhythms.

A different approach to the samba is shown in the next example. The kick, rim, and tom-toms are used to set up a basic two-beat pulse, and the typical samba rhythm is played in the ride pattern. This ride pattern is often played on the bell of a cymbal, imitating the sound of a cowbell.

13
EMBELLISHMENTS
AND
FILLS

RARE IS THE POP SONG THAT RELIES solely on the kick-snare-ride patterns discussed so far. Today's rhythm tracks on pop recordings and in live performance include an array of embellishments and fills that serve to fill out the basic beat patterns, add excitement and propulsion to the music, and signal transitions into new sections of a song. While these variations on basic rhythms are often played on the instruments observed so far—the kick and snare drums, ride cymbal, hi hat, and tom-toms—they may also be stated on additional percussion that expand the palette of drum sounds. Now that we've explored the realm of standard beats in several pop styles, we can move into a discussion of these embellishments and the additional percussion sounds on which they can be played. The libraries of drum machines contain an assortment of sounds that are well-suited for rhythmic fills and variations.

In the last chapter, you used the tom-toms to create certain typical Latin rhythms. Here you'll expand the use of tom-toms in a variety of ways. You'll also develop the use of the hi-hat, creating a distinctive metallic "sizzle" sound by opening and closing the two cymbals. Other sounds either found or simulated on a drum set, added by a percussionist, or included in most drum machines are the rim sound, cowbell, shaker, crash cymbal, and handclaps.

The term "drum fill" comes from the idea of a "fill-in" part in which the drummer plays a busier or louder phrase to move the music from the end of one section of music to the beginning of another. Now drum fills are used quite frequently for a variety of purposes, such as embellishing a musical phrase or building excitement under a guitar solo. Since the possibilities for fills are as unlimited as the imagination of each individual percussionist, it would be impossible to offer here a complete list of standard embellishments. Instead you should use this discussion as a jumping off point for further exploration, keeping in mind that ultimately it will be *your* ear that tells you what is appropriate in the music you're working on.

Tom-Toms. Tom-toms allow numerous ways to create rhythmic and tonal interest in drum beats. Many drum sets and drum machines have three or four tom-toms available with which to expand the tonal variety of any rhythm you happen to be creating.

The four patterns below employ two tom-toms in different ways. In the first pattern, the toms are simply used to "double" the snare drum on the backbeat, creating a thicker backbeat sound. The second pattern uses the toms as though they were a part of the kick drum pattern, thereby providing variation in timbre. The third pattern uses them within the context of kick/snare conversations, again providing tonal variety. The final pattern shows the floor-tom (low-tom) used as the sound for the basic ride pattern, with the eighth-note pulse shown in x's on the floor-tom line. Experiment with substituting toms for cymbals in various ride patterns, but notice how dense this makes the rhythm. Because of its density or bottom-heaviness, this approach should be used sparingly. One possible use is to build up to an instrumental solo over several measures, increasing volume as you approach the downbeat of the solo. In heavy metal music, tom-toms are used more extensively due to the dense "wall of sound" quality of that kind of music.

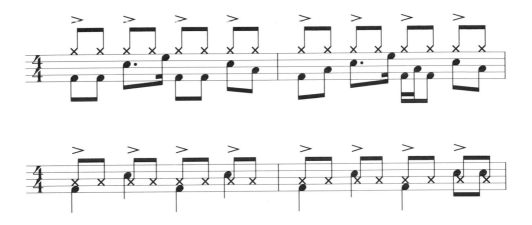

Open and Closed Hi-Hat. It is the unique nature of the hi-hat that it can be played open (by leaving the foot off the hi-hat pedal) and closed (by stepping down on the pedal), allowing for a choice of sounds. An open hi-hat produces a sustained cymbal sound as the two hi-hat cymbals continue to vibrate against each other. The sustain is cut off when the hi-hat closes again, or when the vibration stops. (In the case of a drum machine, the sound may be relatively short due to the length of the sample. With most drum machines, you must program a closed hi-hat note at the point you wish to stop the open hi-hat.)

In notation a tie is used to indicate an open hi-hat beat, which is sustained from the beginning of the tie to the end. The sound will stop at the next closed hi-hat beat.

The closed hi-hat is the most common instrument used for playing the ride pattern. The opening and closing of the hi-hat at certain points in the ride pattern can add a new dimension of sound to your rhythm creations. These examples indicate common uses of the open hi-hat combined with the closed hi-hat within familiar patterns.

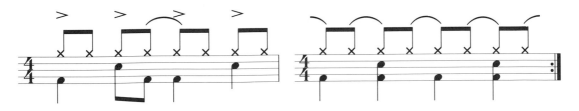

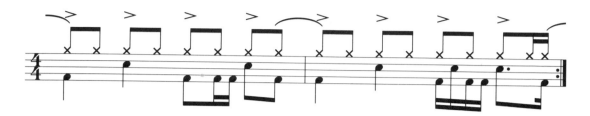

Rim Sound. The sound that is generally labeled "rim" on a drum machine is actually the sound of what drummers call "cross-sticking." This means placing the stick's tip on the drum head and then striking the rim of the drum with the butt end of the stick. It differs from a rim shot, which is a loud sound created by striking the rim and the head of the drum simultaneously.

The rim sound is found on most drum machines and, as you have seen, is especially useful in the bossa nova and other Latin rhythms as it approaches the sound of the wooden claves. Because of its high-pitched, clicking sound, it may also be used as a replacement for the snare drum. The examples below use the rim sound in a few typical beats. These are likely to be used in slower tempos, providing a quieter feeling overall than the use of the snare drum. The rim sound is notated as a ♭.

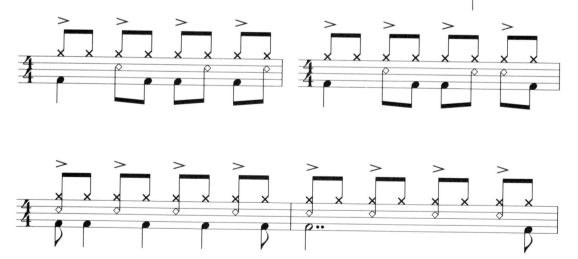

Cowbell. The cowbell has been put to considerable use in most all kinds of popular music, though it is especially evident in Latin-American or Latin-influenced styles. It may serve as an addition to or replacement for the ride pattern, as it has the frequency range of cymbals (but a fuller sound) and like the closed hi-hat, no real sustain. Simple cowbell patterns may supplement hi-hat ride patterns in rock and roll, while complex cowbell syncopation may add spice to dance music in all styles. The examples below show some simple uses of the cowbell, which is written on the second ledger line above the ride pattern.

Shaker. Another instrument in the high frequency range is the shaker, which is often used in direct relationship to hi-hat and/or cymbal ride patterns. It may be used to duplicate the ride pattern, adding texture to the sound. Doubling the ride pattern has an additional benefit in the recording process: it allows you to set up the pattern in stereo by placing the hi-hat on the left channel and the shaker on the right. You can also use the shaker to replace the ride pattern, as in the two-bar example below, or to play an independent idea. As with playing or programming all drum parts, accenting serves an important role in giving the shaker parts a natural feel. In these examples the shaker is notated as an x on the second ledger line above the ride pattern.

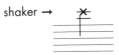

Hand Claps. Clapping has a long tradition in popular music, but the availability of claps on drum machines has made this sound a much more prominent part of many current recordings. (The sound and number of claps in drum machines may vary greatly depending on the model.) Claps are most commonly used to reinforce the backbeats along with the snare, or to sometimes replace the snare. The third example below uses claps within a fill. When using claps in a recording, you might experiment with reverb or digital delay effects to alter or enhance the sound.

hand clap →

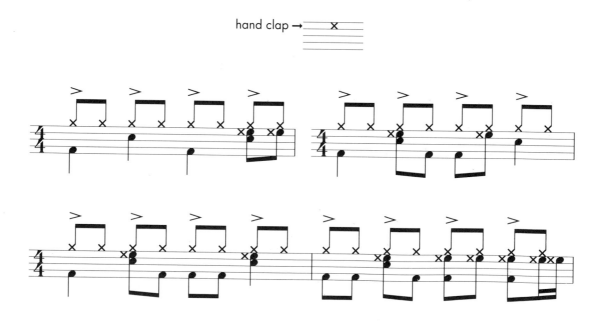

Rock and Roll Fills. Fills are generally used to mark musical transitions, such as a verse moving to a chorus, a chorus to a bridge, an instrumental to a chorus, and so on. Not every (or even necessarily any) transition needs to be marked with a drum fill, but it can be a very effective way to create a strong feeling of movement and arrival.

   The four fills below just scratch the surface of available ideas. The kick drum may or may not play through a fill, depending on what sounds most natural. And normally the ride will stop during a fill as the drummer has to use both hands. (This is not necessary with drum machines, although you'll probably want to try to keep the feeling of something humanly playable.) The point of departure for the fill is important and must be based on the musical context and where the release comes in the other instruments. The fills below will get you started, but you must use your imagination and take your primary cues from the other parts in the overall musical arrangement. In general, short, simple statements will prove most effective in situations that call for fills.

Swing and Shuffle Fills. The following examples illustrate fills from both swing beats and shuffle beats, all employing eighth-note triplets. In the first example, the fill begins before the fourth beat but the snare comes back in on beat 4 to create a normal-sounding backbeat. In the last example, the fill is created by layering first the hi-tom, and then the low-tom with the snare drum.

PART FOUR

DRUM MACHINES AND THE NEW TECHNOLOGY

14
AN
OVERVIEW

THE WIDESPREAD AVAILABILITY AND USE of electronic drum machines is having a tremendous impact on the way popular music is being created, played, and recorded. Today, the full range of drum sounds is at the fingertips of players, writers, and anyone else with an inclination to go out and lay down a couple of hundred dollars or less for a new musical toy. It's no longer necessary for a rhythm creator to be a drummer per se, although it *is* important for guitar players, keyboardists, composers, and arrangers who are making serious use of drum machines to have a working knowledge of the traditional way rhythms have blended with particular pop styles.

There are two parts to understanding how to use a drum machine effectively. The first is knowing how to construct drum rhythms and understanding the logic of contemporary drum patterns. The second is knowing the mechanics of the machine and being aware of all the available applications and programming options. We now proceed to the specifics of drum machine operation and to a close look at other technological developments that are changing the way we think about and create rhythm.

Drum Machines. The drum machine is the focal point of recent technological advances in rhythm. It may be thought of as a combination of a metronome, a library of percussion sounds, and a recorder that, when used as intended, allows us to create complete rhythm parts without playing acoustic percussion instruments. With the recorder we can record any of the sounds in the library into any position along the metronome. The complete range of actions taken to manipulate these elements—to "tell the machine what to do"—is called "programming." We program prerecorded drum sounds into a standard musical format consisting of beats at a tempo (the internal metronome), which is also programmed.

The drum sounds in a drum machine's library of sounds are usually actual recordings of drums, stored as digital information (a digital recording) on a microchip in the drum machine. Earlier drum machines used simulated drum sounds that sounded much less realistic than those of today.

The recorded sounds are triggered by buttons on the drum machine. If you press the snare drum button, for example, the recording of the snare drum sound is triggered to play. In the brave new world of drum machines, pushing the button is roughly equivalent to hitting a snare drum with a drum stick. To make matters more flexible and human, however, newer drum machines include touch sensitivity so that the harder the button is pressed, the louder the sound is played.

When the drum machine is programmed to play various drum sounds in relationship to beats, each sound is triggered each time it is programmed to play. In this way one recorded sound provides all of the sounds necessary to recreate a particular instrument part throughout a composition. For example, the digital chip containing the recording of one snare drum hit is triggered hundreds of times over the course of a long drum machine program, providing all of the snare drum beats used in that program.

Interfacing the Drum Machine. To move beyond the basic programming function of the drum machine you must return to its essentially digital nature. The contemporary drum machine is really a "dedicated computer." The computer part of this term means that it is a programmable electronic device that stores, retrieves, and processes data. It is called a "dedicated" computer because it is dedicated to one essential function—in this case the simulation of a drum set operating in a musical environment.

The drum machine operates primarily within the digital domain, using a simple binary computer language. The digital language of the drum machine enables it to interface with other computers that are programmed using the same (or similar) languages.

This ability has been made possible through the advent of MIDI. MIDI stands for "musical instrument digital interface." It is a computer standard that has been developed to allow digitally-based musical instruments to communicate with each other. Because MIDI is simply a means of connecting devices sharing the same language (of binary digits and digital messages), it is an open-ended system that allows for constantly changing and expanding creative capabilities.

Current MIDI applications are already very broad, affecting almost every aspect of music performance and recording as well as of film and video. For example, MIDI allows one player to trigger several instruments simultaneously, turning him into a virtual one-man band. It also enables that same individual to hook up several instruments to a computer, input their parts and mix them on line, then transfer the mix to a tape recorder in sync with another instrument (such as a drum machine). Newly imagined possibilities are becoming reality on an almost daily basis.

Even before the advent of MIDI, very early drum machines were designed to allow for synchronization with other instruments. By synchronization we mean the ability to link up two or more musical machines to the same tempo. If the machines share the same tempo and beat, they may be used together in the performance of a composition. Yet MIDI has greatly simplified an operator's ability to run numerous instruments simultaneously, and in sync. And synchronization technology is still developing, with current and future expansion closely linked with a time code standard called SMPTE (a form of sync already common in film and video production).

Beyond the Drum Machine. The principles of the basic drum machine have been combined with computer and synthesizer technology to create an assortment of related devices. Among them are electronic percussion instruments that are played like an acoustic drum set—with sticks—rather than programmed. These "controller" instruments, which usually take the form of drum pads, will trigger sounds in the same way a drum machine's buttons trigger its library of sounds. However, the controller pad concept allows access, via MIDI, to a greater number of sound sources. This basic drum machine function—the triggering of a digital sound chip—has become the central part of a much expanded field of electronic drums and percussion, to be discussed in a later chapter.

Another basic drum machine function, the memory of performance information (where and how notes are to be played in relation to the beat), has already been extracted from the drum machine context and used in a different, broader application called a sequencer. In simple terms, a sequencer does for an electronic keyboard what a drum machine does for the library of drum sounds: it allows the user to literally "sequence" the sounds—to program them in a musical environment. For an electronic keyboard, of course, this includes melody and harmony as well as rhythmic information. In a later discussion we will look at some of the broad musicaL applications of sequencers.

The concept of a "sound library" has also been expanded into a very exciting component of the electronic music system: the sampler. A "sample" is a digital recording of an instrument (actually a sample of the sound the instrument makes). While drum machines contain digital recordings (samples) of drums and percussion instruments that may be triggered, tuned, and otherwise manipulated in simple ways, samplers contain digital recordings of potentially *any* sound (musical or otherwise) that can be manipulated in vastly more ways. The advent of samplers and sampling is one of the latest phases in the growing influence of digital technology on musical instruments and music making.

As this process of digitizing, manipulating, triggering, and reproducing sound has become more refined, it has opened up, and perhaps brought us back to, one of the most basic principles of musical rhythm: the human "feel." The question of feel—the idiosyncrasies and inaccuracies of the human performance of music as compared to the mathematical precision of the notational system—has long been considered an essential ingredient in any experience of music.

Drum machines and sequencers have been roundly criticized for their lack of feel. Though part of the problem has been the machines' inability to incorporate elements of feel into a performance, poor programming has been equally to blame. Recent developments, however, have made it possible to program feel into electronic music compositions. They have also provided a much greater ability to analyze the idiosyncratic elements of human performances. We will take a look at ways to manipulate the modern machinery, using time shifting, accenting, swing, and other rhythmic functions, to make the music sound looser, livelier, and more human than the average, stiff-sounding drum machine program.

High technology has had as much of an impact on the contemporary recording process as it has on the development of new musical instruments. Not only has the sound quality improved—thanks especially to digital recording equipment—but entirely new methods of composing and arranging have emerged, which also employ a greatly expanded rhythmic vocabulary. Given the incalculable impact of sound recording on the appreciation and spread of music, it's important to examine the effect of current advances on its capabilities, especially with regard to the recording of drums.

The entire electronic music landscape has changed—and continues to change—dramatically, altering forever the ways in which musicians approach their art and craft. Keeping in mind that today's new rhythmist—now armed with knowledge of rhythm logic, rhythm traditions, and specific beat patterns for particular grooves—is best advised to keep up with the latest developments or be left stranded in the rapidly dissipating dust of low tech, we now embark on an inbound tour through the heartland of the new musical technoscape.

15

PROGRAMMING THE DRUM MACHINE

DRUM MACHINES HAVE SUMMONED UP completely new techniques of making rhythms. There are numerous limitations to drum machines, some of which may be overcome, but there are also tremendous advantages, primarily in the access to rhythm that they are providing to composers, arrangers, and musicians involved in the process of creating and recording music. The term for manipulating the options of one of these electronic rhythm makers is "programming." Programming a drum machine can never be the same as playing a drum set, because the parts are programmed in pieces rather than played all at the same time. In the following discussion we'll take a look at the methods used to program some basic drum rhythms.

Getting Started. We have already described the drum machine's primary functions. To recap, programming a drum machine is the process of using these functions to create drum beats: you trigger various drum sounds from an internal library so that they occur at specified locations in relation to a beat, to assemble full drum set parts for an entire song or composition. Programming is not technically the correct word for the operation of a drum machine since the program is already built into the machines. The drum machine is a dedicated computer that is preprogrammed for writing and replaying rhythm information in the form of drum sounds. What you are doing is simply loading data into the drum machine's program. Nonetheless, programming has become the common term for this activity, and we will continue to use it to describe what is really loading data into a rhythm computer.

The first order of business is to examine the basic procedures of programming, using various simple rhythm figures. While this material is being presented with the assumption that you will be programming as you go along, using a drum machine as you follow the guidelines, it is not absolutely necessary that you do so. If you wish, you may read through the following chapter quickly without immediately putting it into practice. This approach will yield a less-than-thorough understanding of the process, though it should provide a good basic idea of the way drum machines are used and what their capabilities are. It will probably be sufficient for musicians who are not directly involved in the use of these machines and wish to have a better understanding of the new high-tech musical environment.

Drum machines generally employ two basic modes of programming. The first is "pattern," or "sequence," mode in which a short phrase is recorded into the drum machine's memory. These short patterns are the building blocks for the second mode of programming, called "song," or "composition," mode. In this mode the shorter sequences are strung together into complete compositions.

Patterns on drum machines are normally created using one of two different techniques of programming: "real-time" or "step-time." Initially you should try each process. Later you'll be stringing together short patterns to create a song or composition.

The term "patterns" is used because it is standard drum machine terminology for short drum set rhythms (also called "sequences.") It's possible that some of the terminology used here will differ from that used with your particular drum machine. No big surprise; the terms have not yet been standardized. Also, some of the simpler drum machines may not have all of the functions discussed here, while others will have a different basic setup. In general, you may have to make some adjustments for your particular machine. But once the basic concepts are understood, the slight adjustment to a different format is fairly easy to accomplish.

Selecting a Numbered Pattern. Before beginning either method of programming a pattern, it is necessary to select a numbered pattern to work with and to clear it of any previous rhythms programmed into it, usually by means of a simple "clear" function button. Select Pattern 1 (or any other pattern or sequence number in your drum machine) by pressing the corresponding button on your machine, and clear it.

Setting the Framework. Once the pattern is cleared, it must be set up for the basic rhythmic framework of the pattern you will be creating. Usually this is done through two different functions providing various bar length and time signature options. In this case set the pattern for one bar of $\frac{4}{4}$ time.

Finally you must set a tempo, usually given as metronome options listed in beats-per-minute. As you will see, in real-time programming this will be the tempo at which you must play the pattern in order to program it; in step-time programming this tempo is only relevant in playback mode.

Real-Time Programming. In real-time programming you actually play the rhythms into the machine by rhythmically pressing the individual instrument buttons as you listen to a metronome pulse playing at a tempo you have previously selected. The rhythms are recorded into the machine as you play them. This process can be repeated with a number of different sounds from the machine's internal library of percussion samples until you have a fully orchestrated segment of rhythm. This technique resembles normal musical activity in that you actually create the rhythms in "real time" in relation to a pulse. The difference is that instead of striking a drum you are pressing a button and recording the sound into the drum machine's pattern memory for later playback. Another difference is that you are playing the separate components of the drum set at different times.

Setting the Value of the Click. You should have already set Pattern 1 to be one bar long and in $\frac{4}{4}$ time. Next you must set the value of the metronome click that you will use to establish the beat. This may be automatically set to a quarter note in your drum machine or you may have the option of using a different note value for the click (though the $\frac{4}{4}$ time signature defines the beat as a quarter note). Generally the quarter note will be the easiest beat to program with, though for complex rhythms it is sometimes easier to use an eighth-note click. For these rhythms set the click to a quarter note. Then select any tempo between 80 and 100 beats-per-minute. The one-bar pattern will continuously repeat in both programming and playback modes. The quarter-note click will establish the pulse and the beat, acting as a rhythm guide for programming.

Quantizing. Finally, you must set the level of quantizing before you program the pattern. Quantizing represents the most radically different musical capability that drum machines offer. Generally, quantizing means setting the smallest note value that is available to be programmed at any given time. Quantizing has somewhat different functions in real-time and step-time programming, though they are closely related. In real-time programming quantizing operates as an auto-correct function (also called error-correct or timing-correct).

Say you set the quantizing function for a quarter note value. This means that quarter notes are the smallest subdivisions of time available for programming. In real-time mode this means that any note played will be "corrected" to sound on the nearest quarter note to the point when it was played. Thus, if you play a snare-drum beat (strike the snare button) between beats 2 and 3, the machine will move that snare beat to the nearest of those two beats when replayed.

Quantizing greatly simplifies the programming process because you don't have to perform the rhythm perfectly; you may approximate the performance and the machine will correct it to the smallest note allowed by quantizing. You may also program part of a pattern using one level of quantizing (say, eighth notes) and then switch the quantizing (to, say, sixteenth notes) for programming another part of the pattern. Quantizing does not affect the playback once the part has been recorded. If a six-teenth-note part is played using a sixteenth-note level of quantizing and then the machine is switched to an eighth-note level of quantizing, the sixteenth notes will play back as they were initially recorded (though you can't program sixteenth notes with the quantizing function set to eighth notes).

In real-time mode it is also possible to turn the quantizing function off. In this case the machine will simply record the rhythm exactly as you play it—at the exact moment the instrument button is pressed in relation to the beat. Actually, the machine is still quantizing, but at such a high level of resolution—usually 192 divisions per beat—that the effect is essentially that of an accurate reproduction of the notes' placement.) Programming without quantizing can be very tricky but can also yield some of the most natural-sounding results—all the quirks of human fallibility are allowed into the program. Triplets are also available in quantizing, though they are usually referred to by their mathematical equivalent rather than their proper name, e.g., a twelfth note rather than an eighth-note triplet.

Inputting a Pattern in Real Time. As an initial approach to programming, we'll consider two simple drum set rhythms. These are patterns based on the rock and pop beats discussed in Chapter Nine. For the sake of simplicity, they are one-measure patterns; two-measure patterns are also common building blocks for drum set parts.

To record the following pattern in real time, you should begin by setting the quantizing function to an eighth note. Because this is the smallest value used in this pattern, this will enable you to program all of the parts most easily.

PATTERN 1

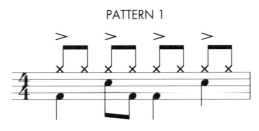

Start the drum machine in the real-time mode. You should be hearing the metronome clicking in quarter notes. Usually the 1 beat is distinguished by a different sound as the measure repeats around and around. There is a normal playback mode in which no programming can take place and whatever has already been programmed is playing back. If you are not hearing the metronome beat, you may be in playback mode instead of real-time programming mode. Refer to your manual or use trial and error to get into the proper real-time function.

The ride pattern is most commonly played as a closed hi-hat sound. The ride pattern in this beat is straight eighth notes, so tap the closed hi-hat button continuously over the one-bar pattern. Because the quantizing function is set to eighth notes, it is impossible to program too many hi-hat beats into the pattern. And even if you play the hi-hat unevenly, quantizing will force it into even eighth notes. Once all the possible eighth notes have been entered, you will have the eighth-note pulse shown in the pattern.

Next, program the kick drum by pressing the kick drum button on the 1 beat, on the "and" of 2 beat, and on the 3 beat, as shown in the above pattern.

Now program the snare drum for the 2 and 4 beats. Remember that all you must do is play these parts close enough to the proper beat, and the quantizing function will move them to the correct location. Once they are played, the drum machine remembers their location and retriggers them each time the measure repeats.

Clearing a Pattern. If you make an error in programming, or decide that you wish to change the pattern in some way that means eliminating something you have already programmed, you must use the clear, or erase, function. Usually you can erase pieces of your pattern by holding down the clear button and then pressing the desired instrument button during the real-time input function. You must press the instrument button so that the timing matches that of the note to be cleared. Usually the clear button is also used to erase entire patterns or entire instrument parts within a pattern. Both of these functions are done in the rest mode—when you're not inputting—rather than during real-time programming. By using the clear function and by reprogramming, you can edit your patterns until you have the rhythm exactly as you wish.

The Copy Function. One of the most useful of all the drum machine functions is the copy function. This allows you to copy one pattern into different pattern number locations for use in creating a longer program. This is helpful because patterns are often very similar to each other, and it is much easier to begin with a programmed pattern and then edit it than to start from scratch for each new pattern. In order to program Pattern 2 (below), begin by using the copy function to copy Pattern 1 into the drum machine's location for Pattern 2. Once you have done this, you may edit Pattern 1 (not the original, which is still located at Pattern 1, but the copy, which is now located at Pattern 2). You are going to edit Pattern 2 so that it ends up sounding like this:

PATTERN 2

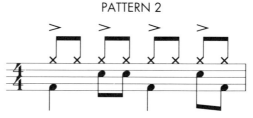

Editing a Pattern. In order to edit Pattern 1 into Pattern 2, it is necessary to add one snare-drum beat, and then clear and add one kick-drum beat. Beginning with the snare, you must simply add the "and" of 2 beat. The same "and" of 2 beat must be cleared from the kick drum pattern, and the "and" of 4 beat must be added. All of this editing must take place while the machine is playing in the real-time mode. Once you have edited the pattern to play as above, stop the machine and use the normal playback mode to check Patterns 1 and 2. You should be able to switch back and forth between the two patterns (in playback mode, not in real-time mode) and listen to the transition from one to the other.

Step-Time Programming. With step-time programming, drum machines (and their more cumbersome predecessors) have introduced an entirely new technique for creating rhythms. Here rhythms are created out of the context of normal musical time. The machines are set to "step" through the pattern at a specific rate. For example, you can set a drum machine's metronome for a one-bar pattern, and the stepping function at eighth notes. You may then "step through" the bar one eighth note at a time, advancing the pattern by pressing the appropriate stepping button. At each eighth-note location, you may add or delete any voice from the library of sounds by pressing the instrument button. Rhythms are then played back "in time" to the musical beat, at the tempo you have set. Thus you can create rhythms without any of the physical coordination of a drummer, without even coordinating the pressing of buttons in time to the beat. In fact, *anyone* can create complex or "unplayable" rhythms. This computer-assisted programming technique represents what has to be the most revolutionary technical development in the history of rhythm.

In step-time programming, the quantizing function is used to select the rate at which you may step through the pattern. Different levels of quantization may be used to program different parts into one pattern. For example, you may program eighth-note rhythms (as in the above patterns) by setting the quantization to eighth notes and then stepping through each eighth note of the one-bar pattern, loading sounds into their appropriate locations as you go. You might then reset the quantization to sixteenth notes and add a sixteenth-note part to the pattern.

Real-time programming may also be combined with step-time programming in the creation of one pattern. It is often more efficient to input the simple parts of a pattern in real-time mode and then switch to step-time for loading a particularly tricky passage.

Inputting a Pattern in Step Time. Pattern 1 may be loaded using step-time mode after setting the pattern length to one bar, the time signature to $\frac{4}{4}$, and the quantization to eighth notes.

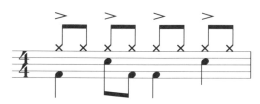

Start with the ride pattern. Step through the measure and at each eighth-note location press the closed hi-hat instrument button to load the ride rhythm into the pattern.

When you've returned to the 1 beat, step through using rests (usually by simply pressing the step button without pressing any instrument buttons) until you get to the 2 beat and load a snare drum in that location. Step through three more eighth-note rests to the 4 beat and add the second snare drum backbeat at that location.

Then step one more eighth-note rest back to the 1 beat and load the kick drum pattern into the appropriate beat locations. The tempo you have selected will not affect this process until the pattern is played back.

Different machines have different methods of step recording. On one model you first set the step record mode, then you select the instrument. After this you press buttons indicating note and rest values for the entire measure (for that instrument). Then you go back and input each instrument in the same way.

Editing a Pattern in Step Time. Editing a pattern using step-time programming usually uses the same technique as with real-time, though again it may be accomplished out of musical time. You may step to the location where you wish to delete an already loaded sound and then, by pressing the clear button and the instrument button together, that sound will be removed from that location. Similarly you may return to any location via step-time and add another sound not previously programmed.

To create Pattern 2 from a copy of Pattern 1, you simply delete the kick drum beat from the "and" of 2 and add a kick drum beat on the "and" of 4. You then step through the pattern again, and when you are back at the "and" of 2 beat you add a snare drum.

It is valuable to become familiar with both real-time and step-time modes of programming, as each is especially useful in different situation for different musicians. Using only one mode or the other will tend to limit the kinds of rhythms you are likely to program.

Real-time programming is probably most valuable for loading simple rhythms, as it allows you to hear what you are creating as you go. Step-time programming, however, is especially useful for complex rhythms and for subtle manipulations of the beat.

Song Mode. Once you are comfortable with creating patterns or sequences, you must master the song, or compose, mode that most drum machines employ. This mode allows us to string patterns together to create longer and more involved compositions or songs. Song mode resembles the "cut and paste" options found on many different computer software programs that offer word processing and graphics capabilities. As with cut and paste, there are various options from which to choose in working through this basic form of programming.

Programming a Song. In order to program a song, you must first find the song mode function (usually a single button selection) and, just like programming a pattern, select a numbered song to program—say, Song 1. You must then clear that song number of any previous programming and enter the edit mode, again using a single button selection.

When you edit a song, the basic functions will be insert, delete, and repeat. Normally, after entering song edit mode, you will begin with Part 1 and will insert into it the pattern you've decided to put first. (A "part" is essentially a programmed "compartment" into which you can insert a pattern that can then be manipulated, moved, or copied into various sequences.) Once a pattern is inserted into Part 1, you may then proceed to Part 2 and enter another pattern. By repeating this process, you construct a series of patterns which become the parts of a continuous song form. The delete function allows you to remove a pattern from a specific part number. The repeat function allows you to repeat a pattern rather than having to insert it, from scratch, into many consecutive parts. When you activate the repeat function, you need to enter the number of repeats for the part selected, and the number of the part where the repeat is to begin.

Using insert, delete, and repeat allows you to construct and then edit the sequence of patterns that will make up the song structure. This process can become quite involved if the song you're working on contains many sections such as an introduction (intro), a verse, a chorus, a bridge, vamps, alternate verses, solos, "outros," and so on. Keeping in mind that verses, choruses, and other sections might eventually contain more than one drum pattern, you begin to see that your song may require a quite complicated rhythm part. However, the various sections are generally closely related and may be relatively easy to program once the basic patterns have been created.

You have written two different patterns in the previous sections of this chapter; let's call Pattern 1 a verse pattern and Pattern 2 a chorus pattern. In song mode you might link these patterns together into an alternating verse/chorus song form. If the verse were eight measures long and the chorus four measures, you would create a song form that inserted Pattern 1 into Parts 1 through 8 and then inserted Pattern 2 into Parts 9 through 12, repeating these sections according to your plan for the format of the song. You can also program this by inserting Pattern 1 into Part 1 and then repeating Part 1 seven times, then inserting Pattern 2 into Part 2 and repeating it three times. In this case, the first eight measures will all be Part 1, and the next four measures will all be Part 2.

Creating More Patterns. To make a more interesting drum program for your song, it will be necessary to create many more patterns similar to Patterns 1 and 2. First you must create new or alternate patterns for different song sections (such as the intro) and then program them into the song parts. A list of activities that would yield appropriate patterns might run something as follows:

• Create Pattern 3 for the intro. First take Pattern 1 (the verse pattern) and copy it to Pattern 3. Then edit Pattern 3 by deleting the ride part and then entering a new ride pattern based on quarter notes. (You could also do this by clearing all of the "and" beats in the ride pattern.) Then add a bass drum beat on the "and" of 3. The resulting intro pattern should be as shown.

PATTERN 3 (Intro Pattern)

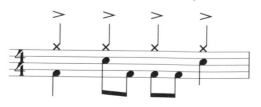

• Create an alternate verse pattern by copying Pattern 1 to Pattern 10 (or any open pattern number you wish). Edit Pattern 10 by adding a kick drum beat to the "and" of 3 and a snare drum beat to the "and" of 4. These additional notes add a little more movement and interest to the rhythm. The resulting alternate verse pattern should be as shown.

PATTERN 10 (Alternate Verse Pattern)

• Create an alternate chorus pattern by copying Pattern 2 to Pattern 20 (or any open pattern number). Edit Pattern 20 by adding snare drum beats on the "and" of beat 3 and the "and" of beat 4, and delete the kick drum beat from the "and" of 4. These additional snare notes also add movement to the basic chorus pattern and may be used as a fill. The resulting alternate chorus pattern should be as shown.

PATTERN 20 (Alternate Chorus Pattern)

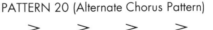

• Create a fill to go from the intro to the verse by copying Pattern 3 (the intro pattern) to Pattern 30. Edit Pattern 30 to contain a short snare drum fill as shown below. In order to program the sixteenth notes in this fill, it will be necessary to quantize Pattern 30 to sixteenth-note lengths.

PATTERN 30 (Intro Fill)

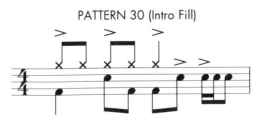

Let's say that the final song form is going to be as follows: intro, verse, chorus, verse, chorus, double intro, chorus, chorus. (Songs may certainly contain many more parts than this.) In this arrangement you are using a double intro toward the end of the song in place of a bridge or a solo. You have not programmed an ending.

The alternate patterns you edited can be used to make the program more interesting and more natural sounding. A final programmed song form that would employ these patterns, within the simple song structure outlined above, would be something like this:

Bars 1–4	Intro	Part 1	=	Pattern 3 (intro pattern) *Repeat Part 1 two times*
		Part 2	=	Pattern 30 (intro fill)
Bars 5–12	Verse	Part 3	=	Pattern 1 (verse pattern) *Repeat Part 3 six times*
		Part 4	=	Pattern 10 (alternate verse)
Bars 13–16	Chorus	Part 5	=	Pattern 2 (chorus pattern) *Repeat Part 5 two times*
		Part 6	=	Pattern 20 (alternate chorus)
Bars 17–28	Verse and Chorus			*Repeat from Part 3 one time*
Bars 29–36	Double Intro	Part 7	=	Pattern 3 (intro pattern) *Repeat Part 7 six times*
		Part 8	=	Pattern 30 (intro fill)
Bars 37–44	Double Chorus	Part 9	=	Pattern 2 (chorus pattern) *Repeat Part 9 two times*
		Part 10	=	Pattern 20 (alternate chorus) *Repeat from Part 9 one time*

There are numerous choices for the location of these patterns, as well as many other related patterns and fills that you might have created and used. The ability to restructure the overall song form is an especially valuable tool for arranging. You can try different arrangements without losing the original by copying the song to another song number and editing the newly created version into a different arrangement. Most drum machines also provide a song chaining function that allows you to link several songs together to set up smooth transitions between songs when using the drum machine in live performance.

Organization is the key to the effective use of song mode. Most drum machines have limited display capabilities, so you must keep track of the patterns and song form in order to see the whole form at once. (See Chapter Seventeen for a discussion of personal computer programs that expand drum machines' display capabilities.) Writing down what each pattern is to be used for and outlining the complete song form (in terms of sections such as verse and chorus) is generally a necessary supplement to the memory of the drum machine.

Other Functions. Drum machines provide numerous other functions beyond basic pattern and song programming. An important function for programming natural-sounding rhythms is accenting. Setting up different volume levels for different notes within a pattern can make your mechanical rhythms sound much more human. Control over accenting varies considerably between different drum machines.

Another available control that pertains to feel is known as the swing function, which allows you to place beats in other than the traditional musical locations (eighth notes, triplets, sixteenth notes, and so on). The swing function is really a form of quantizing, but the notes are placed in between normal values—between a proper eighth note and eighth-note triplet, for example. This function is in recognition of the fact that in natural human performance, notes are intentionally displaced from their mathematically proper location in order to provide the rhythm with a looser feel.

The area in which drum machines tend to differ from each other the most is that of the library of sounds. This function differs in terms of both the quality of sound and the number of available percussion instruments, such as shaker, tambourine, cowbell, and handclaps. Many machines provide several choices for the basic kick and snare drum options. Others allow you to edit the sound and tune its relative pitch. Some drum machines even give you the option of recording your own sounds and adding them to the preset library. These functions generally become more elaborate in packages that separate the sound portion of the drum machine from its programming portion.

Other programming functions may include individual instrument level and output assignments. Some drum machines have a stereo output, allowing you to assign a degree of panning from left to right for each of the sounds within a stereo image. Certain machines enable you to assign different instruments to different outputs, providing a greater degree of control over the processing of individual instruments sounds (to be discussed in the context of recording in Chapter Nineteen).

Memory storage is another important function in drum machines. Because a drum machine's memory is limited, you must be able to download it to some other medium (allowing it to be retrieved later), thus freeing the memory of the drum machine for new programming. Drum machines typically can handle three to ten songs in their memory. Other media to which you can download memory include a cassette, a synth data cartridge, or a floppy disc.

An additional function of drum machines is synchronization, allowing you to play the machine in sync with other electronic instruments and tape recorders. As we'll see in the next chapter, both storage and sync functions have been enhanced by the advent of MIDI.

As you begin to work with drum machines, bear in mind that mastery comes only with a good deal of practice. Working back and forth between programming, listening, editing, and refining will eventually provide you with the skill necessary to begin programming complex rhythm parts without spending all day doing it. Try to avoid getting stuck in one method of programming. Use all the functions available to you, including both real- and step-time programming, various levels of quantization, and the copy and edit approaches to song building. And experiment with rhythms; bring your own judgment into play and get to the point where creating original rhythm parts on a drum machine becomes a natural and comfortable process.

16

MIDI, SYNC, AND A BUYER'S GUIDE

AMONG THE MOST WIDELY IMPLEMENTED innovations in the development of digital technology has been an interface that allows synthesizers, drum machines, and computers to communicate and to function together. The advent of MIDI (an acronym for musical instrument digital interface) has brought about an across-the-board change in the way musicians can approach the performance of their music and use drum machines as part of a system of electronic components. A key function in the communication of separate pieces of equipment is synchronization, which refers to the process in which different timing elements run together "in sync" in musical time. It may use MIDI as well as other standardized communication protocols. The following is intended as a basic introduction to the concepts of MIDI and synchronization.

MIDI. MIDI is a standardized digital interface that is used in almost all current synthesizers and drum machines. It is also starting to be incorporated into many audio processing devices and personal computers. This interface allows different instruments to communicate with each other, regardless of manufacturer. A standardized MIDI plug-in port allows for the connection between MIDI-equipped instruments and computers.

The digital language transmitted via MIDI has been designed to communicate certain elements of musical performance. It is made up of building blocks that function like words in spoken language. They are basic units of musical performance information, based on the starting and stopping of sound. The equivalent of notes and rests in the language of MIDI are messages indicating note-on and note-off occurrences. A part of MIDI language also includes protocols for the transmission of data. These protocols may be thought of as similar to language conventions such as capital letters and punctuation marks. MIDI is a highly expandable, software-based system that has already found many different applications.

The MIDI port is simply a five-pin DIN plug—a West German standard connection system designed to accommodate five wires. Generally there are three MIDI ports on each instrument: MIDI IN, MIDI OUT, and MIDI THRU. MIDI IN is for receiving a signal which contains MIDI messages from another MIDI instrument. MIDI OUT is for transmitting MIDI messages, and MIDI THRU is another output that transmits a direct copy of messages that come through the MIDI IN port.

The most basic and common use of MIDI is in the connecting of two or more synthesizers so that more than one synthesizer will sound when only one of the keyboards is actually played. A typical setup might appear as follows:

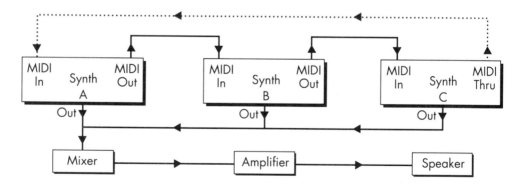

This configuration shows several different options, which should be clear from following the connections. If synthesizer A is played, then the performance information will be transmitted from MIDI OUT of synthesizer A to MIDI IN of synthesizer B, causing it to sound. If synthesizer B is played, messages will be sent out of synthesizer B to the MIDI IN of synthesizer C, causing it to sound. The messages coming in to synthesizer C will also be sent out of its MIDI THRU port to synthesizer A, so that when synth B is played, all three synthesizers will sound. When synth C is played, it will be the only synth to sound, since it has no MIDI OUT port connected to another synth. Although certain variations can occur (for example, the

MIDI OUT is sometimes selectable as a MIDI OUT or a MIDI THRU), this diagram illustrates the basic principles of MIDI port connection.

The ability to play two or more synthesizers simultaneously via MIDI is sometimes referred to as "triggering": the keyboard from one synth triggers another via the MIDI connection. The ability to trigger performance information via MIDI allows for another important capability. You may divide up primary components of synthesizers and drum machines and then connect the component of one unit with a different component of another. For example, you may use the keyboard of a synthesizer with a sound module located elsewhere, with the keyboard triggering the sound module via a MIDI connection. A sequencer (such as computer software and a PC linked with a synth keyboard) can be programmed for a drum beat and then used to trigger the drum sound in a separate sound module via MIDI. A basic setup would appear as follows:

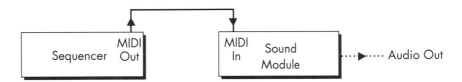

MIDI employs two basic kinds of messages: channel messages and system messages. Channel messages contain basic musical performance information—note-on/note-off messages sent from a keyboard or sequencer to a sound module. Note-on/note-off messages may be triggered by depressing the keys of a keyboard or MIDI programming devices such as drum machines and sequencers. Pressing the key of a keyboard or the button of a drum machine sends out a note-on message to whatever sound module it's connected to, thus triggering the actual sound. Other performance messages transmitted on channels are touch sensitivity (keyboard velocity), program changes corresponding to patch numbers on synthesizers, pitch bending, aftertouch, and control changes such as on/off for vibrato, portamento, or damper pedal.

Channel messages are so named because they may be sent on any one or all of sixteen different channels. The channel system operates similarly to the broadcasting of TV transmissions, where a TV is receiving all of the broadcasting channels but is only responding to the channel it is set to receive. In MIDI, different sound modules may receive different performance information from the same source, and through the same connection, by employing different channels for different information. The various modules must be set to the appropriate receiving channel. The user controls this by setting up particular "mode" messages. These contain transmission protocols such as "omni" mode, meaning information is being sent on all sixteen MIDI channels. If omni mode is off, then the transmission must be sent over one of the sixteen MIDI channels. Other kinds of mode messages are "poly," meaning "polyphonic" (more than one note at a time), and "mono," meaning "monophonic" (one note at a time). Thus there are four possible MIDI modes as follows:

The Four Modes   1 omni on, poly   2 omni on, mono
                              3 omni off, poly   4 omni off, mono

System messages do not use channels, as they control the entire system. System messages include synchronization information, and protocols which allow a machine to interface with a personal computer. The computer must be programmed to understand the protocols employed by a particular machine. Computers also require a MIDI interface to allow the computer to receive MIDI messages. (Some computers are now being made with built-in MIDI interfaces.) When equipped with a MIDI interface and programmed to be compatible with a particular device, a computer may be used to expand the memory and operation of the machine (discussed further in Chapter Seventeen).

For the drum machine user, the MIDI interface has proven to be a real boon, allowing you to extend rhythm capabilities in a number of directions: via MIDI you can increase both the machine's memory and the number of sounds it's capable of controlling. In addition, MIDI controllers—that is, devices that generate musical performance information via the language of MIDI—are being perfected for almost all kinds of musical instrument activity. MIDI guitar controllers have been very difficult to perfect due to the mechanics of the guitar, but manufacturers are beginning to find ways to deal with all the various problems. The same is true of wind controllers such as saxophones and clarinets. It seems likely that, before long, MIDI controllers will be available to translate virtually any kind of instrument sound into MIDI information and thus allow the player access to unlimited sound sources.

While MIDI has opened up vast new possibilities in the creation and control of sound and performance, there are also problems with this new technology. The most significant one is the speed at which the system works. There are very short delays in the transmission of MIDI data. The more complex the MIDI setup, the more pronounced the delays may be. These timing delays can make MIDI unusable in some applications, though various interfaces have been developed that maximize the transmission of data and make even very complex MIDI setups workable. Some technicians also complain that MIDI is not sophisticated enough to accommodate the kinds of developments that are likely to occur as technology advances. Eventually the MIDI standard may be replaced, but it currently represents one of the most powerful and important elements in the new technology of music.

Synchronization. Synchronization involves linking the timing of two or more elements so that they run together in musical time. For example, you may wish to run two drum machines together to create one part and thereby access both libraries of sounds at the same time. To do this, the internal metronomes (or "clocks," which form the basis of the beat) must be in sync with each other. This is accomplished by using the clock from one of the machines to drive the others, commonly called a master/slave relationship. The master clock performs the timing function for the other machines which are slaved to it. The machines run in sync because they are running off of the same clock. We may use several machines in this fashion with one master clock and many slaves. Tremendously complex performances may be synchronized in this manner.

The synchronization of clocks may occur in several different ways, and MIDI has tended to simplify the process. Prior to MIDI, the interfacing of clocks was made difficult by the different clocking rates and kinds of connectors used in different machines. MIDI, on the other hand, puts out a simple kind of clocking signal as a system message, which is standardized for all MIDI equipment. To synchronize two MIDI-equipped drum machines, you simply connect the MIDI OUT from one of the drum machines (whichever is chosen to be the master) to the MIDI IN of the other machine (which will operate as a slave to the clock from the master machine). The slave machine will have to be programmed (usually by a simple function switch) to receive and clock to external MIDI clock pulses. When the master machine is started, the slave machine will also start, running to the clock of the master. Any number of MIDI-equipped drum machines and sequencers may be run in sync to the master clock.

Another important kind of musical synchronization involves getting the drum machines and sequencers to work in sync with standard tape record-ers. We refer to this process as "sync to tape." In its simplest form, we record the clock from one of our machines on to one track of a tape recorder. This clock, now recorded on tape, becomes the master clock as the tape is played back, driving all of the machines as slaves. It allows you to create parts on a drum machine, then sync the drum machine to one track of a multitrack tape recorder, and then record other parts in sync to the drum machine by overdubbing on other tracks of the tape recorder.

MIDI clock cannot be used as a signal to record on tape, and normal clocking data used between machines is also not reliable when recorded on tape. Various sync-to-tape standards have been used, the most common of which is called FSK. An FSK tone acts as a simple master clock, providing timing information to drum machines and sequencers that are capable of receiving this particular format. Again, the machines must be set to receive this tone before they will slave to it.

The problem with simple MIDI clock sync and basic tape sync is that they are not "intelligent" synchronizing systems. What this means is, be-cause they can only recognize the most basic kind of clocking information, they aren't able to communicate anything other than the timing of the beats. In contrast, more advanced kinds of clocking information also pro-vide data on relative locations of beats. These systems can provide infor-mation to a drum machine or sequencer about the location of any par-ticular beat in relation to the beginning of the song or composition. This allows the user to play back entire systems in sync beginning at any point in the song, rather than having to always start at the beginning of the song in order to achieve sync.

The most common type of "intelligent" clock is SMPTE time code. SMPTE (an acronym for Society of Motion Picture and Television Engi-neers) is the time-code standard developed in the film and television industries to synchronize audio to video and film cameras and editors. The widespread use of drum machines and sequencers has made SMPTE very useful for synchronization in purely audio contexts as well. Other time codes that have recently been developed include a "smart FSK" tone that provides location as well as timing information. MIDI is also capable of responding to these "intelligent" time codes through two different MIDI protocols. One is "MIDI song-pointer," and the other is a new format, closely related to SMPTE, called "MIDI time code." Both of these MIDI system messages can transmit location information to drum machines and sequencers that have the capability to receive them.

Because of all the various standards that have been developed for synchronization, it is clear that there is no real standard at all. Even with MIDI, the technology continues to evolve so that older machines may be compatible with most MIDI operations but may be unable to respond to more recent MIDI protocols. The uses of SMPTE and similar "intelligent" time codes are a rapidly expanding part of the new technology.

A Buyer's Guide. Having explored drum machines and their MIDI-linked extensions, we now move to a discussion of what to consider when shopping for equipment. New models of drum machines seem to appear on the market almost daily as manufacturers scramble to keep up with the competition. Shopping for drum machines, like most anything else, requires an understanding of what is available and what is important to you, the "end user." Since a survey of individual models would be an extensive undertaking and would probably be outdated within a short period of time, the best advice about what to look for in a drum machine would have to focus on features. The following list of questions may serve as a sort of "buyers' checklist of features" for prospective drum machine purchases. This survey will also serve to outline and review previous topics pertaining to the operation of drum machines.

Programming or Sequencer Operation. Does the machine program in both real time and step time? Is there a display for patterns that have been programmed? What is the smallest level of quantization available in either mode? What accenting capabilities are included? Is there a song or compose mode? How many editing features does song mode support? Can you chain songs together for live performance?

Library of Sounds. How many sounds are available in the machine's voice library? What is the quality of sounds used—do you like the way they sound? Are the sounds tunable? Are you able to load other voices into the machine's library of sounds? Is there a sampling option for user-created sounds?

MIDI and Sync. What different clock rates are available for synchronization? Is the machine MIDI-equipped? What is the extent of MIDI implementation (how many different kinds of MIDI messages are available to control)? How effectively can you trigger other drum machines and synthesizers via MIDI? Does the machine support MIDI/SMPTE lock-up, especially MIDI song pointer or MIDI time code? Does the machine read or write SMPTE?

Other Features. Can you trigger sounds from any source other than MIDI (such as from drum pads, or from tape)? How many separate outputs are there for the library of voices? Are there computer software programs that expand the memory and usability of the drum machine? (Keep in mind that adding outboard sequencers and samplers will add considerable expense.)

The better your understanding of the capabilities of drum machines, the easier it will be to pick out the machine best suited to your intended use, within the available budget. Shop carefully, read those specification sheets, grill the sales person, and be sure to play with the machines in the store before buying.

17
ELECTRONIC PERCUSSION, SAMPLERS, SEQUENCERS, AND COMPUTERS

UP TO THIS POINT, OUR DISCUSSION of the new wave of electronic instruments has focused on the drum machine. This machine actually represents only one specific use of the technology that made it possible. Basic drum machine technology has opened up other expanded techniques for creating rhythm, such as new means of playing and programming electronic instruments. At the same time, the personal computer has become part of the new tech music environment as a result of the MIDI digital standard. The following discussion explores these provocative new technologies.

Electronic Percussion. Along with drum machines, electronic drum sets that are actually played rather than programmed have become a common replacement for, or addition to, the traditional drum set. (Today's record producers quite often supplement a live drummer with electronic percussion sounds.) Electronic drum kits normally consist of drum pads which can be struck with a stick like an acoustic drum. The pad itself makes almost no sound, but triggers a sound which is produced by a module linked to the pad. Usually, the triggered sound is subject to the velocity of the attack on the pad so that it reflects changing dynamics. The sound module or "brain" usually consists of a variety of drum sounds similar to those in a drum

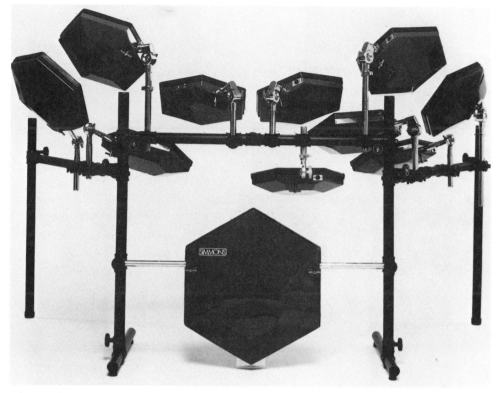

Electronic drum set

machine's sound library, along with various other percussion voices. In its early forms the drum pads and sound modules used several kinds of electronic pulses to trigger the sound. This limited the possibilities for interfacing: only pads and sound modules manufactured by the same company could be used together, adding up to a closed system. MIDI has opened up the system, with all MIDI-equipped drum pads able to trigger MIDI-equipped sound modules, regardless of manufacturer.

Prior to the use of digitally recorded drum sounds, the sounds of an electronic drum were synthesized using "analog" technology. Analog sounds start with a tone generator and simulate drum sounds by manipulating a simple tone. Tones are created using different kinds of sound waves, which produce different qualities of sound (timbres). Other kinds of sounds, such as "white noise" (a combination of all the frequencies) may also be mixed with the tones. The basic characteristics of the tone are manipulated by altering what is called the "envelope" of the tone. The envelope includes the relative volume and duration of the attack, sustain, decay, and release (ASDR) of the tone. The pitch of the tone may also be altered, while retaining the basic timbre of one instrument. By altering only the pitch, for example, it is possible to simulate various sized tom-toms from one tom-tom sound.

Analog drum sounds tend to have a characteristic "electronic" timbre which is identifiable as synthetic but at the same time is authentic enough to pass for the sound of real drums. They have been most commonly used to *supplement* the acoustic drum set rather than replace it entirely. Drum pads are often used in place of tom-toms or other sounds such as hand claps or special effects.

More recent developments allow for several different triggering sections on one drum pad. Each section of the pad represents an independent trigger, so that several different sounds are available. It is even possible to change the sound triggered by any individual drum pad or section of a pad, meaning that many more options are available here than on a normal drum set. And different sounds may be called up for different songs. The drummer is limited only by the number of voices in the sound module's library, and because these may be edited and altered, the potential may be limitless. Drum machines have generally been programmed to imitate standard drum and percussion sounds. The sound modules of electronic drums, on the other hand, are capable of simulating a much broader array of drum instruments as well as other noises and special effects. But the sounds, however limitless in concept, are still synthetic in tone and limited to the general production capabilities of the module. Fortunately, new innovations have taken us far beyond these synthetic analog sounds, and even beyond the digital recordings of standard sounds found in most drum machines. These innovations come in the form of what is generally called a sampler.

Samplers. The latest technology in drum machines and synthesizers allow user sampling. Sampling is simply the process of digitally recording a sound into a machine and thus adding it to the library of available sounds. Thus we might record a particular drum, or percussion instrument, or trash can lid, or dog barking, and then use that as a sound to be programmed into a rhythm sequence or triggered from a pad.

A sampler may come equipped with a keyboard, or it may simply consist of a sound module that must be triggered via MIDI from an external source such as a keyboard, drum pads, or a sequencer. Sampling with keyboard synthesizers allows sounds to be recorded and then played back within the normal pitch range of a keyboard. The sampler translates the recorded sound (the sample) so that it can be played throughout the normal pitches in the chromatic scale. Just as synthesizers can produce the sounds of other instruments such as acoustic piano, strings, or horns, so can they reproduce custom-sampled sounds and play them back with the pitch capabilities of a normal keyboard instrument.

Drum machines are also being made that allow user sampling—the addition of new sounds to the drum machine's library. These samples can't be manipulated with the flexibility of keyboard/synthesizer samples, but then, drum and percussion uses may not require a lot in the way of variation.

The options provided by various samplers differ enormously, though the key feature of any sampler is the quality of the digital recording used to create the sample. As with so much of the new technology, the ability of the sampler to be expanded through interface with a personal computer is an important element in its use.

Sequencers. Drum machines, as we have seen, provide the ability to access a potentially unlimited library of sounds. We can manipulate the sounds into endless arrangements and combinations using a digital recorder that can set and remember location, duration, velocity, and other programmable information, all in relation to an internal metronome-like clock. A similar relationship has developed between digitally-based keyboard synthesizers and recording devices called sequencers. Sequencers record and replay a performance through any MIDI-equipped synthesizer. We can also program this kind of performance in step time and replay it in real time as we do with drum machines.

Sequencers take many different forms, such as the sequencer section of a drum machine, which has been the focus here. Sequencers have also become common additions to keyboard synthesizers, built right into the computer architecture of the synthesizer. These sequencers, usually called "on-board" sequencers, will drive, via MIDI, other synthesizers as well. Personal computer sequencing software has also been developed, offering various advanced capabilities. There are also "dedicated" sequencing computers.

Sequencers do not actually record musical sounds; they simply record the digital performance data generated by a musician playing a synthesizer.

As with the drum machine, we set up a pattern, or sequence, and the internal clock establishes the musical beats in that pattern. The sequencer then remembers note-on and note-off information, meaning the sequencer keeps a record of when any given notes on the synthesizer keyboard were depressed and released in relation to the beats of the pattern. When we replay the sequencer it actually "plays" the synthesizer by turning notes on and off in the same relationship to the beats of our pattern. The sequencer also remembers other performance information, such as the velocity with which the key was struck, translated into volume dynamics. Other synthesizer functions such as pitch blend, modulation, and aftertouch are also recorded as performance information.

As already pointed out, the basic functions of a drum machine may be separated into a sequencer (recorder) and sound module (library of sounds). The sequencer repeats, or replaces by programming, the actual playing function. Keyboard sequencers differ from the sequencer sections of drum machines in that they deal with pitch and sustain information. This requires additional functions as well as more thorough editing control. Drum and keyboard functions are now being combined into single sequencers. This means that most sequencer sections on drum machines now follow the keyboard sequencer format, using *keyboard* note assignments for individual drum or percussion instruments. Thus the snare drum is assigned to a specific note on a keyboard. You may also trigger the drum sound from notes on the keyboard of a synthesizer via MIDI.

Sequencers not only provide a new means of recording music, they also offer new approaches to composition and performance. The functions of step-time recording and error-correction, or quantizing, for example, allow users to compose, perform and record far beyond their physical abilities. Editing functions such as cut, copy, and paste allow new flexibility in working out compositions and arrangements, easing the process of moving sections of music, or reworking melodies. Sequencers also allow expanded control over transposition and other harmonic and melodic functions. These extraordinary programming and editing capabilities have allowed for performances and musical manipulations that were previously impossible.

Sequencers are being used more and more in live performance situations. Live musicians play along with preprogrammed sequencer and/or drum machine performances. This has enabled bands to recreate, in live shows, the sequenced synthesizer and drum machine parts used in their recordings, a feat that, some years back, was out of reach without hiring numerous auxiliary musicians. One of the limitations of these electronically enhanced performances is that live musicians must follow the timing established by the sequencers. Current technology, however, promises the ability to run the clocks of the sequencers and drum machines directly from the timing of a live performance by one of the musicians, most likely the drummer.

These new methods of programming and recording have been made widely available through the advent of MIDI. Prior to the acceptance of the MIDI standard, sequencers were cumbersome and simplistic, though they were certainly in use and their potential was being widely discussed. Alongside MIDI, the personal computer has played a significant role in the development of sequencer technology.

Computers. The development and refinement of computer technology have generated many of today's innovations in sound. The majority of the electronic instruments and machines discussed so far are, in fact, computers. As discussed earlier, they are what is called "dedicated" computers, because they are dedicated to very specific tasks such as the sequencing function of a drum machine. The amount of computing power within each machine sets the limits of its capabilities. MIDI, however, has enabled us to expand the functions of dedicated computers by providing a link to much greater power—the power of a personal computer.

For a personal computer to connect to a piece of electronic gear it is necessary that it have a MIDI interface. (Some computers are equipped with built-in MIDI connections.) The MIDI interface (purchasable as a discrete item) provides MIDI ports that can send MIDI messages into the computer's memory. The MIDI interface must be compatible with the particular computer, as different computers use different protocols for receiving digital information.

You must also have computer software that allows for the desired interaction with the musical equipment. There are many varieties of software, and they are of two general types. One provides broad MIDI functions such as sequencing, and generates MIDI channel information that can interface with all sorts of MIDI equipment. The other type is geared toward one particular piece of MIDI equipment and uses system messages that are specific to that piece of equipment. Both add considerable power to the general process of using MIDI-equipped musical gear.

Types of Software. There are four basic kinds of music software currently in use. They may be generally classified as providing sequencing, scoring, editor/librarian, or sound designer capabilities. While each of these functions are different, they also may interact or be combined in various programs. What *all* of these programs provide is expanded power through additional computer memory, excellent display capabilities on the computer's monitor, and fast and convenient storage and retrieval. (Some software is available for several different makes of computers, while other software is intended only for specific makes and models.)

The earlier discussion of sequencers touched on the topic of "on-board" sequencers, so-named because they reside within a particular synthesizer. Among the drawbacks of these sequencers are their limited editing and display capabilities. Drawing on the power of a personal computer, sequencing software has been developed that erases earlier limitations. Computer sequencing software works in the same way as the sequencers discussed previously, and is capable of driving any MIDI-equipped sound module. Along with drum machine sequencers, on-board sequencers, and personal computer sequencing software, there are also a number of dedicated sequencers on the market. These sequencers have the same general functions as the software programs, but they are "dedicated" because sequencing is the only function that they perform. They generally include disk drives and plenty of computing power for editing, but they usually lack the display capabilities of a personal computer's monitor. Their advantage is that they are less expensive than a personal computer and monitor, MIDI interface, and software. Obviously, they have none of the non-musical applications available on a personal computer.

Scoring programs allow various levels of music transcription that can ultimately be printed out as sheet music or musical scores. Editing functions include cut, copy, paste, and musical transposition. Lyrics may be inserted along with musical markings such as bar numbers and rehearsal numbers. These programs may provide additional convenience features such as verification of rhythms to time signatures and of pitch ranges for specific instruments.

One of the more remarkable features of certain scoring programs is the ability to enter musical information directly from a keyboard. A musical (or simply rhythmic) passage played into the computer via MIDI will be translated into musical notation. Working in the other direction, you may also play compositions that have been scored in the software by sending them via MIDI to a synthesizer. In this way scoring programs are similar to sequencers. In fact, some of them do include complete sequencer capabilities, while other ones can interface with sequencing software to accomplish the same basic functions.

Simple librarian software allows the memory from MIDI-equipped gear to be stored on a personal computer's disk system. This type of software uses the system messages that are unique to a particular piece of equipment. Librarians are most commonly used to store specific patch data from a synthesizer, or memory from a drum machine or on-board sequencer. This provides faster and more reliable storage than you can get on a cassette, more storage space than is available from data cartridges, and greater display capabilities than provided by the instruments themselves. These librarians are often combined with editors that offer similarly increased flexibility in the editing of synthesizer voices or patches. Also available are voice libraries that provide numerous patches for specific synthesizers. In today's marketplace, editor/librarian software generally appears at the same time that new equipment is released.

While voice editors provide expanded access to the functions of a synthesizer, sound designer programs offer even more control over samplers. The digital recordings that are a central part of samplers can be manipulated to a high degree when you use the power and display capabilities of a personal computer. This software combines access to subtle aspects of sound creation, such as wave forms, with advanced editing capabilities. Again, the software must be written for a specific piece of equipment to make use of its proprietary MIDI system messages.

At the high end of the market, some manufacturers offer complete music computing systems which combine sampling, sound designing, sequencing, scoring, and editing. These self-contained, dedicated computer systems offer the ultimate control over the infinite variables of music composition and performance.

At the cutting edge of current computing technology is what is termed artificial intelligence, or AI. AI attempts to recreate the human rational process as applied to music creation. In software this has taken the form of random sequence generation to invent synthesizer voices. While these haven't found much use so far, they probably point the way to future applications of computer power to musical activity.

18

ADVANCED PLAYING AND PROGRAMMING

THERE IS NO SUBSTITUTE FOR REPETITION, whether you're practicing stick exercises on a drum or programming a drum machine. Once you have mastered the basics, you must combine programming skills with knowledge of how a drummer plays to create drum beats that sound natural.

The biggest complaint about drum machines is that they sound *unnatural*, meaning they sound mechanical and inhuman. There are two subtle ways of manipulating your rhythm programming so that this mechanical sound is replaced by more natural-sounding rhythms. The first of these is accenting; the second is shifting of time values.

Accenting. Interestingly, it is not the "perfect" time of the drum machine that is primarily responsible for its mechanical sound. It is a lack of accenting that will most obviously distinguish a machine from a live drummer. Fortunately, drum machines usually have an accenting function that can help to alleviate the stiff, mechanical feel. Numerous examples of accenting in pop rhythm can be found in the examples in Part Three. Here we look at the accenting options provided in drum machines and sequencers.

There are four basic types of accenting available in rhythm programming. (1) The first is a universal function that provides one accenting variation with one preset increase in volume, applied across-the-board to all instrument sounds that occur on a given beat. This means that an accent programmed on the 1 beat will accent all instruments programmed to play on the 1 beat, and it will increase the volume of all those instruments by a fixed amount. (2) The second type allows individual accenting by instrument, though the level of the accent is fixed. This means that you may accent the kick drum on the 1 beat but retain an unaccented hi-hat on the same beat. The amount of accenting, that is, the increase in volume used to create an accent, remains constant whenever it is applied to any given instrument. (3) The third type allows you to vary the amount of accenting applied to a particular instrument. For example, you may accent the kick drum by one amount and the hi-hat by another. In this case, however, the degree of accentuation remains constant on each individual instrument for all beats on which the accent is applied. (4) In the fourth kind of programming, there is control over all the possibilities. This means accenting by individual instrument, with level options for each note of each instrument independently.

This fourth level of accenting control will allow you to create the most natural-sounding rhythms. When a drummer plays a drum set, the volume of each note of a performance will vary slightly. Though this amount of complexity is generally too much to attempt in a programming procedure, small variations in level on certain notes can create a very natural feel, even with mechanically perfect time.

Let's say you have ten levels of accenting available for every given note. With an eighth-note hi-hat pattern, you would probably start by accenting each quarter note beat of the pattern. If you make each accented note a level 7 note and each unaccented note a level 3 note, then the levels for one measure of $\frac{4}{4}$ would read 7, 3, 7, 3, 7, 3, 7, 3, corresponding to the eight eighth notes. You might then create small variations in the accented and unaccented notes so that the final levels might read 8, 3, 6, 2, 7, 3, 6, 4. This would provide the natural variations that might occur if the part were played on a drum set.

MIDI has generally allowed more flexibility in the application of accents through programming. Most computer-based sequencers provide the fourth type of accenting capability. Now, drum machines are also providing this flexibility either through programming or the use of touch-sensitive pads or buttons. The touch-sensitive pads enable you to play the rhythms into memory (either quantized or not), and the harder you strike a note the louder it is played and recorded. Each note will be programmed at a different level, depending on the strength with which the trigger pad has been struck.

In your experiments with accenting to obtain a natural feel, you might want to program some of the rhythms presented in Part Three. Although these examples show different levels of accenting, further variation of volume levels will provide even greater expression of the "human" element in drumming.

Shifting Time. The shifting of time values is another means of reducing mechanical feel, but it is more difficult to control or program. Few drum machines are designed to allow this subtle a manipulation. However, many machines do provide a "swing" function, which can offer a limited kind of time shift. Layering of delayed sounds is another means of time shifting that is usually available. The most sophisticated approaches usually require an external sequencer or a personal computer and programming software. Time shifting can also be programmed relative to certain synchronization techniques, especially when using SMPTE time code. We will look at these advanced techniques and how they are being used to provide subtle changes in the feel of rhythms.

The term "swing" has been primarily associated with jazz, and has been used to describe a particular era in jazz history. The word has also been applied in a purely descriptive manner, as in the way we might characterize a band or a piece of music as "hot." The qualities which make some performers hotter, or swing harder, have been much debated and discussed. A certain consensus has developed that pertains to a particular kind of time shifting, and this function, often labelled "swing," is provided on many drum machines. The traditional swing beat in jazz is expressed in the following ride pattern:

The two "ta" triplet beats (the "ta" of 2 and the "ta" of 4) create the skeleton of the triplet subdivisions that are prevalent in swing rhythms. It is through time shifting of these triplet embellishments that we express the swing function. The manipulation of swing has generally been thought of as the process of pushing the "ta" triplet beat closer to the following down beat. When done in extreme, the triplet may become an "a" sixteenth note instead. Thus the basic jazz rhythm is sometimes written (and sometimes played) as a sixteenth-note rhythm.

Even though this rhythm may be played as the ride pattern, the use of triplet subdivisions is most likely to occur in the rhythms of accompanying instruments. Interestingly, jazz rhythms are often written using straight eighth-note subdivisions, with the application of a "ta" triplet (or even an "a" sixteenth note) being assumed as the appropriate interpretation. Thus the basic ride pattern may be written in eighth notes and played using either triplets or sixteenth notes.

These variations imply a flexible approach to the placement of the "ta" triplet, and this is what is at the heart of swing. The placement of the "ta" beat may be time-shifted so that it occurs anywhere in the space between a straight eighth note and a sixteenth note (or even closer to the following beat). Thus the possible location of this swing beat embellishment may fall anywhere in the space shown.

In drum machines these swing beat variations are usually expressed in percentages. We program the beat as straight eighth notes and use the swing function to move the intermediary eighth note closer to the following down beats. Thus a swing function of 50 percent maintains the straight eighth note (50 percent is halfway between the two downbeats, thus equal to a straight eighth note). A swing function of 67 percent (technically 66⅔ percent) would be equal to the true "ta" triplet as this is two-thirds of the way from one downbeat to the next. At 75 percent the straight eighth note has become a true sixteenth note.

The swing function usually provides additional options between a straight eighth note and a "ta" triplet, such as 54 percent, 58 percent, and 63 percent, and perhaps one option between the "ta" triplet and the "a" sixteenth note at 71 percent. These percentages create notes that cannot be expressed using the standard notation system (unless extremely small note values are used), and they allow a greater degree of expression in the rhythms you create. When the "ta" triplet is moved closer to the following downbeat a tighter, bouncier, more hard-swinging feel is created. When the "ta" triplet is held back closer to the preceding eighth note, a more relaxed, looser feel is created. The ability of musicians and programmers to adjust rhythms in this way is a central part of expressing feeling in music.

While the swing function relates to the placement of what are essentially embellishment notes, or subdivisions of the main beat, the placement of actual beats may also be manipulated using time shifting. In basic rock and pop, this will mostly happen on the snare drum backbeats (beats 2 and 4). The kick drum beats on 1 and 3 become the control beats that define the mathematical time. The 2 and 4 beats may then be moved either in front of the beat or behind the beat. In front of the beat means the snare actually plays before the mathematically correct 2 or 4 beat; behind the beat places the snare just past the mathematically correct locations. Generally, before the beat creates a more driving kind of feel, behind the beat provides a heavier, more "grooving" kind of feel.

Time-shifting effects must be created using very small movements or they will simply sound like errors. Most drum machines, and even many sequencers, do not provide small enough note values or increments of quantizing to allow this kind of time-shifting. Variations of this kind are better expressed in milliseconds than in note values because the note values would have to be so small to be usable (when do you really deal with a 256th note?). Consistent variations in the placement of the backbeat may be created by delaying the snare drum with a digital delay (or by using a MIDI delay). This would allow you to delay all the backbeats by five milliseconds to create more of a "groove" feeling. Moving in front of the beat might be a little trickier, though it could be accomplished by programming the snare on the sixteenth note before the 2 and 4 beats and then delaying it until it is only a few milliseconds before the actual 2 and 4 beats, creating a more driving feel.

Naturally these effects are going to be easier to create if the sequencing software has very small increments available for time shifting. This is becoming more prevalent, especially as SMPTE and MIDI time codes, which do use small increments of time, become the basis for clocking information in sequencers. By programming very small time values, we can also produce a randomizing kind of time shifting. This would involve shifting many notes of all the instruments both in front of and behind the beat, thus reflecting the natural idiosyncrasies of a human performance, which will never always be in sync with mathematically perfect time. These effects should be created with time-shifting equivalents of just one or two milliseconds in either direction, or the feel will sound merely sloppy.

There are other interesting aspects of time shifting. Notes placed behind the beat will tend to be less insistent, and complex parts may serve a more natural, less disruptive function when played or programmed in this way. On the other hand, notes before the beat will push harder and call attention to themselves, perhaps providing a needed lift to a particular phrase. Drum fills, often used to move the music from one section to the next, may suggest the direction of movement by being slightly behind the beat when moving to a quieter passage, or slightly ahead of the beat when going to a more driving section. This brings up the question of using time shifting consistently through various sections of a song or composition. Sometimes it is effective to approach each section differently. You may lay back on the verse and then push the chorus, for example.

Sequencing of instruments other than drums may also contribute to a much more natural-sounding feel in programmed music. Musicians have always incorporated time shifting into their playing, consciously or not.

Technology is beginning to provide the tools that allow this kind of extensive subtlety in programming. It is also providing the means to quantify information from human performances. We are now able to measure and analyze the exact amount of time shifting employed by a performer in a given performance. When this is done a kind of map is created showing the position, relative to the beat, of each note played. This map can be used to drive the rhythms of a sequencer program, effectively (though not necessarily appropriately) translating the feel. Only a few relatively expensive devices can carry out this function, though it is an increasingly common feature in computer sequencing software. It is an area that will continue to develop and is likely to provide valuable applications of AI (artificial intelligence). By using AI, for example, we may be able to reinterpret performance information to create randomizing time shifting that reflects specific musical or individual styles.

Imitative Versus Non-Imitative Approach. When programming rhythms into a drum machine, the user has a choice to make: whether to consistently try to create patterns that are playable by a real drummer, or whether to ignore "real life" playability and instead generate rhythms that are possible only on machine. This decision will have an important impact on how natural the final rhythms sound.

There are many limitations to the rhythms a drummer can play on the drum set, primarily due to the drummer's limited number of limbs. When a drummer plays a tom-tom fill, for example, he or she must naturally stop the hi-hat pattern in order to free the hands for the fill. When you program a drum machine, the hi-hat pattern may continue to play during the fill. If you stop the hi-hat pattern for the fill, you are using the imitative approach, programming what would be natural and necessary for the drummer. If you allow the hi-hat to continue to play during the fill, you are using the non-imitative approach.

The question of imitative versus non-imitative most often arises when you are programming drum fills. But it is also a general issue in the creation of complex rhythms that may be technically impossible to play but can still be programmed on drum machines and sequencers. There is no right or wrong answer to whether the imitative or non-imitative approach should be used, but you should be aware of the differences and apply whichever approach sounds and feels the best to you.

It is not only in programming that "impossible" drum parts can be created. Today's recording techniques allow drummers to play parts that would be impossible to play all at one time. This means that live drummers may use the non-imitative approach to drum fills by overdubbing parts after the original rhythms have been recorded. Nonetheless, non-imitative drum parts may still sound unnatural and should be used only when the music seems to benefit from this approach.

19
RECORDING RHYTHM

As we have seen, the current technological revolution has had a huge impact on the composition and performance of music and its underlying rhythm patterns and drum parts. It has also had a powerful effect on music reproduction and recording. Drum machines, synthesizers, sequencers, sync, time code, triggering, and sampling may now all be part of the music reproduction process, and their use represents a significant departure from traditional recording technology. The "old-fashioned" approach to recording has also undergone some remarkable changes in the past several decades.

The basic procedures for recording and processing music have altered radically since the earliest attempts at sound recording. They have been greatly enhanced by the introduction of new recording consoles, tape recorders, and signal processing devices that allow incredibly accurate reproductions of musical sound.

The now-standard multitrack tape format, for example, enables an engineer to assign instruments to different channels, thus providing the ultimate degree of control over the volume and tone of a band's individual elements. Complex performances can be captured and remixed to yield recordings of great depth and clarity.

The basic sound quality of today's recorded music has been vastly improved by new developments in equalization (tone control), compression, and expansion (noise gating). These processes have been particularly effective in the recording of the drum set, offering wide flexibility in the choice of timbre and in the isolation of individual instruments.

Further refinements to processed sound are made possible by sophisticated units that can simulate acoustic environments and produce both natural and intriguingly unnatural effects. Among them are digital delay and reverberation (reverb) units, and these can also serve as powerful rhythm-creating devices. Through timed repetition of sound created by delays, you can generate fantastically complex arrays of rhythm and music. Basic room ambience, now controllable with digital simulations, greatly affects our perception of rhythm.

New recording techniques create new challenges for drummers as well as for composer/producers who work with rhythm tracks. In the following discussion, we'll focus on various aspects of the modern recording process, especially as they pertain to rhythm. Of primary importance are (1) the initial recording, (2) equalization and signal processing, and (3) mixing.

The Recording Process. Multitrack tape recorders have revolutionized the recording process. They come in many formats, defined primarily by the number of available tracks. Standard formats are four-, eight-, sixteen-, and twenty-four-track machines. Popular four-track tape machines are now widely available in cassette as well as reel-to-reel formats.

The key to multitrack recording is the ability to selectively choose between record and playback functions for individual tracks from the same record/playback tape head. You may record on track 1 of a four-track tape recorder and then play it back while recording on track 2. The two tracks will be synchronized because they are adjacent to each other on the same piece of tape crossing the same tape head. Thus as you are listening to track 1 you may be recording in sync on track 2. When tracks 1 and 2 are played back together, they will sound just as they did as you were recording track 2.

This process of simultaneously recording one track while playing back a previously recorded track is generally referred to as overdubbing. Parts of tracks may also be recorded in this manner, using a technique called "punching in and out." Say you have overdubbed track 2 in sync with material already recorded on track 1, but there was a mistake in one section of the material on track 2. You may place track 2 in the record-ready mode and begin playback, monitoring both tracks 1 and 2. At a point prior to the error on track 2, you begin recording on this channel only (punching in) and replace the section containing the error. At a point after the error, you deactivate the recording process (punching out). In this way music can be assembled in very small sections with great editing capabilities.

Most popular music is created using a multitrack tape recorder. Thus performances on a single composition may be recorded at different times, by the same or different people, ultimately adding up to a complete composition. At the professional level, a twenty-four-track recorder, providing twenty-four independent channels for recording, is the standard. Music may not only be composed in stages, it may now be recorded in stages as well. It may be, and in fact often is, composed, arranged, and recorded using this method.

For the drummer and percussionist, the ability to overdub and the availability of many tracks has radically altered the recording process. Today, most popular music recordings are made using a click track (a simple metronomic pulse) as a rhythm guide, recorded onto one track of the multitrack tape recorder. The click track serves as the basic pulse and tempo of the song. The drum track must be played relative to this metronomic pulse. This generally proves to be both a challenge and an advantage for the drummer.

Learning to record to a click track can be difficult depending on how much practice a musician has had with playing to a metronome and how difficult the percussion part is. Some drummers find that playing to a simple drum machine part is easier than staying with a click track. In either case you do not want to waste expensive time at a recording session learning to keep up with a metronomic pulse. Therefore, ample practice at home or in the practice studio are essential to preparing for this type of recording. It is also very important that the click track, or whatever is used as the guide track, be loud enough for the drummer to hear it comfortably. This can often be a problem because the drums themselves are quite loud (and, in fact, generally sound best when played loud). The drummer must insist that the volume be turned up on the guide track.

As you saw in the previous chapter, "feel" is very important to the rhythmic quality of a piece of music. Playing to a click track does not eliminate the responsibility of providing an effective, musical approach to rhythm. The drum performance may, in fact, vary slightly from the exact pulse of the click track and thereby provide variations in rhythmic feel.

While the click track acts as a guide for the drummer, the other musicians generally follow the drum tracks. This is because the drums are what end up on the final recording and because the "feel" of the drum track may differ from the strict metronomic pulse of the click. Usually other instruments such as the bass, rhythm guitar, and/or keyboards are recorded at the same time as the drums. While these instruments may be replaced (rerecorded) later, it is helpful to the drummer to hear them in addition to the click track. These parts remind the drummer of the feeling and structure of the composition. The other instrumentalists may also *detract* from the drummer's ability to create the proper feel and may even make it difficult to remain in sync with the click track altogether. When only the drummer is playing to the click while the other musicians follow the drums, it is important that they be comfortable with metronomic time or they will be likely to push or pull the drummer away from the pulse. It is best to rehearse this approach—the rhythm section playing together while the drummer plays to a click track—*prior* to going into the recording studio.

Many new recording techniques have opened up to drummers as a result of click tracks and the flexibility of overdubbing. Thanks to the click track, it is possible for drummers to record or rerecord their parts after other instruments have been recorded. Sometimes recordings are made to click tracks or drum machine parts, and live drums are added later on in the process, using the click or machine sounds as guides. In some cases only the basic drum parts—the kick drum and snare drum—are recorded initially. Other parts of the drum set, such as hi-hat and cymbals, or tom-toms, are added to separate tracks later. Multitracking and overdubbing allow you to record individual elements of the drum set onto different tracks, also making it possible to substitute specific elements later in the recording process. As previously discussed, these parts may be replaced with different sounds by triggering drum machines or samplers. Live drums may also be used to replace parts by simply rerecording an instrument (such as a kick drum) separately onto a track of its own.

Drum miking and tracking (the assigning of various pieces of the drum set to separate tracks of the multitrack recorder) have also evolved. Individual microphones for each component of the drum set and separate tracks for many of the elements have become part of the standard technique for drum recording. Generally the kick drum, the snare drum, the hi-hat, and individual tom-toms are recorded with separate microphones, while the cymbals are recorded using two overhead mics that create a stereo image of the cymbals. Sometimes "room mics" are placed far from the drum set to capture the ambient sound of the drums in the room. A common tracking layout provides separate tracks for the kick drum, the snare drum, and the hi-hat, with two tracks used for a stereo image of the tom-toms and two tracks used for the stereo overhead (cymbal) mics. Room mics may have their own track (or two for a stereo image), or may be mixed onto the same tracks as the overhead mics. Among the many benefits of this procedure is the fact that it allows broad flexibility in the application of signal processing.

Equalization. Equalization (EQ) or tone controls provide the most powerful tools for the processing of sound. EQ allows you to selectively boost or attenuate (cut, dip) various frequencies and thus alter the sound quality. The application of EQ to drums and percussion is a critical part of the recording process.

To understand EQ you must first understand the division of sound into frequency bands. Frequency refers to the number of sound vibrations per second, with fewer vibrations producing lower pitches, and more frequent vibrations producing higher pitches. When we divide the sound spectrum into frequencies from low to high, we use Hertz (Hz) as the unit of measurement. One hertz is equal to a frequency of one cycle per second. The human ear is capable of hearing sound between approximately 20 Hz and 20 kHz (1 Kilohertz = 1,000 Hertz). We generally divide the frequency range into three categories: lows (low frequencies), mids (midrange frequencies), and highs (high frequencies). Vibrations increase in frequency across the sound spectrum so that the number of Hertz in the high frequencies is far greater than in the lows. As shown in the following chart, these general categories tend to overlap:

lows: 20 Hz to 400 Hz
mids: 250 Hz to 2 kHz
highs: 1 kHz to 20 kHz

EQ units come in a wide variety of types, some of which are built into recording consoles. The primary features of EQ controls are boost/cut, the center frequency, and the bandwidth. The boost/cut control either increases or decreases the center frequency, which is the Hertz setting for that particular EQ control. The bandwidth is the breadth of frequencies above and below the center frequency, which are also affected by the boost/cut control. The simplest varieties of EQ offer only boost/cut control, with the center frequency and bandwidth preset. For example, an EQ knob marked "highs" will boost or dip high frequencies, usually up to plus or minus 12 dB (decibels—a measurement of volume in a given frequency range). The center frequency and bandwidth will be preset. A common highs EQ setting might be a center frequency at 5 kHz and a bandwidth of 2 kHz above and below the center frequency. A common application of high-frequency EQ would boost up to 6 dB, with the primary boost at 5 kHz and the actual boost covering a range from approximately 3 kHz to 7 kHz as shown below.

HIGH EQ TONE CONTROL

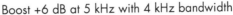

Boost +6 dB at 5 kHz with 4 kHz bandwidth

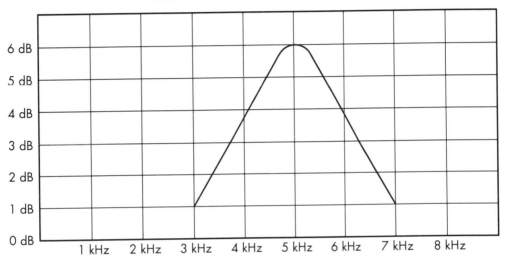

The most common kinds of EQ are fixed frequency, stepped-frequency, sweep, and parametric. Different EQ configurations may have different numbers of bands. The number of bands refers to the number of controls available within the full range of frequencies. The simplest EQ is usually two-band fixed-frequency EQ. This would generally take the form of two rotary knobs, one marked highs and the other lows. The highs knob would allow 12 dB of boost/cut with a fixed center frequency (usually between 3 and 8 kHz) and bandwidth. The lows knob would offer the same degree of boost or cut with a fixed center frequency (usually between 60 and 120 Hz). Three-band fixed-frequency EQ with the addition of a mids control is becoming increasingly common. Graphic EQ is a form of fixed-frequency EQ that employs sliding faders rather than rotary knobs and usually allows for a larger number of bands. A twelve-band graphic EQ allows boost/cut at twelve different fixed-frequency locations.

Stepped-frequency EQ usually employs one rotary knob for boost/cut and a switch that allows for the selection of different center-frequency positions. For example, a stepped-frequency EQ may have a lows boost/cut knob and a switch that selects either 60 Hz or 120 Hz as the center frequency. The control for highs may include a switch for 3 kHz, 5 kHz, or 8 kHz.

Sweep EQ is becoming increasingly common in the EQ sections of recording consoles. In each band there will usually be two rotary knobs, one for boost/cut and one sweeping through the center frequency locations. For example, a lows EQ section will have a boost/cut knob and a sweep knob that allows continuously variable selection starting at 40 Hz and sweeping through the frequency range up to 500 Hz. Three-band sweep EQ would provide boost/cut and sweep functions in each of the three main frequency ranges: lows, mids, and highs, usually providing some overlap between ranges. The bandwidth remains constant for each center frequency selected. Sweep EQ is commonly configured as a single rotary knob with a separate inner (boost/cut) and an outer (sweep of frequencies) control.

Parametric EQ provides control of all three major aspects of EQ: boost/cut, sweep of frequencies, and width of bandwidth. It is the same as sweep EQ, but has the added control of bandwidth, sometimes as a stepped function (i.e., three bandwidth selection switches providing broad, normal, or narrow bandwidth) and sometimes as a continuously variable sweeping function (a rotary knob that sweeps from broad to narrow bandwidth). Some sweep and parametric EQ allows for what is called "shelving," rather than a width of bandwidth control. Shelving creates an asymmetrical bandwidth curve. High-frequency shelving will boost all frequencies above the center frequency equally, and low-frequency shelving will boost all frequencies below the center frequency equally. High-frequency shelving is often desirable on sounds that include a lot of high frequency information, such as snare drum and cymbals.

Other types of EQ featured on elaborate recording console/mixers may include low- and high-band pass filters. Low-band pass filters allow all frequencies below the selected frequency to pass unaffected while all frequencies above the set frequency are heavily attenuated. For example, a low-band pass filter set to 10 kHz allows all frequencies below 10 kHz to pass while all frequencies above 10 kHz are cut. A high-band pass filter provides the opposite effect. For example, a high-band pass filter set to

100 Hz allows all frequencies above 100 Hz to pass while all frequencies below 100 Hz are heavily cut. You might use a high-band pass filter on the overhead tracks in drum recording, thereby cutting out the boom of the bass drum while allowing the cymbals to be unaffected.

The use of EQ will vary greatly depending on the nature of the original sound source and the subjective ear of the user. Understanding a few basic EQ principles will assist in its application. Human hearing has a natural EQ bias of its own. While the ear picks up between 20 Hz and 20 kHz when functioning at its best, it hears the midrange frequencies more effectively than the highs or lows. The ear is biased toward the midrange because these are the frequencies of the normal speaking register; it is where we get our primary information. Musical sounds, on the other hand rely heavily on the highest and lowest parts of the audible frequency spectrum for their timbre (tone quality). It is the high and low overtones produced along with the basic sound (the root-note frequency) that give the sound depth, richness, and its unique tone quality. Thus the natural bias of the ear tends to cut out some of the more pleasing aspects of tone. Most EQ work is done to compensate for the ear's natural bias. It centers on enhancement of the high and low frequencies that fill out the musical timbre of a sound, to which our hearing is not well-attuned. Thus the most commonly applied EQ curve will be the inverse of the natural frequency bias of the ear.

COMMON APPLICATION OF EQ CURVE

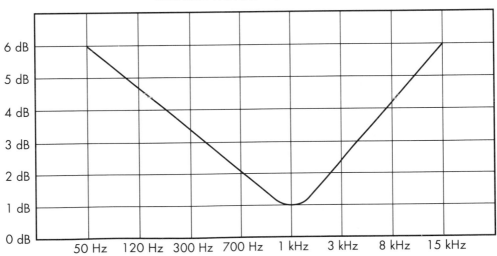

Many audio receivers have a "loudness" function, designed for low-level listening enhancement. The loudness effect is no more than an EQ curve applied to the overall sound. The curve boosts both the lows and the highs. This loudness curve corresponds to the common EQ curve shown above, emphasizing the inverse of the ear's natural EQ bias. Notice that while this effect is most commonly achieved by boosting high and low frequencies, a similar effect may be achieved by cutting mid frequencies. Using mid-frequency cut can be an effective alternative to this normal EQ curve, especially when high-frequency boost is adding or increasing unwanted noise.

Drums respond well to EQ, especially to the common EQ curve employing high- and low-frequency boost and/or mid-frequency cut. It is useful to think of the sound of a drum in two parts when applying EQ. The first part of the sound is the attack, sometimes called the "tick" or "click" part of the sound. This is the part of the sound caused by the stick hitting the drum head. A more prominent attack will cause the drum to be more audible and distinct from other instruments and sounds. A boosted attack has become especially common on kick drum sounds, but it is also useful on tom-toms, conga drums, timbales, and other drums. The attack may be made more pronounced by increasing the high-frequency EQ, centering on the sound of the attack. Sweep or parametric EQ will allow you to locate and boost the best-sounding part of the drum attack; in a snare drum, this is called the "crack" portion of the sound.

The second part of the sound of a drum is the body, or the resonance, which is the sound of the drum resonating after the head has been struck. This part of the sound responds well to low-frequency EQ boost and also may be cleaned up and enhanced by mid-frequency cut. Low-frequency boost will add body and tone to the sound. Low-frequency boost on a snare drum will increase the "fatness" of the sound, but may also add an undesirable tone or "note." Some people enjoy the "note" in the snare drum, and its use is subject to taste.

Hi-hat and cymbals contain more high-frequency information than most musical sounds. They will often respond well to some additional high-frequency boost in the range of 10 to 15 kHz. Because they contain so little information below the mid frequencies, it may be desirable to cut the low frequencies as much as possible just to eliminate noise or rumble, and, in the case of recording live drums, to minimize leakage from the drums into the cymbal and hi-hat microphones.

Signal Processing. Signal processing refers to the myriad ways in which sound is altered and adjusted during the recording and mixing of music. The most powerful kind of signal processing is the application of EQ. A second type is level or gain control, which pertains to various means of altering the natural volume of a sound (dynamics). Compressors, limiters, and noise gates are all types of level controlling devices. Another kind of processing involves the addition of ambient effects. Such powerful tools as digital delay and reverb units recreate the natural echos that occur in the acoustic space of a nightclub, a concert hall, or even the Grand Canyon.

Level controlling devices are used widely in the recording process for several reasons. Recording devices are much more limited than the human ear in their ability to effectively process a wide variation in volume. They are limited in the quiet range by what is called the "noise floor" (the various sounds, hums, and hisses that are by-products of much technology), and in the loud range by distortion. Modern techniques of noise reduction and digital recording have reduced these problems, but the process still lags behind the human ear. Devices such as compressors and limiters (a limiter is really just a compressor with less tolerance) reduce the dynamic range by cutting back the volume of any signal that passes above a certain threshold. The compressor may be adjusted to different thresholds, and the ratio (degree of compression above the threshold) can be set. By reducing the dynamic range the signal is less likely to distort at high volumes and less likely to get lost in the "noise floor" at low volumes.

Compression may be used on a vocal, such as an announcer or a singer, or it may be applied to any instrument as a means of maintaining a consistent and audible level throughout a piece of music. Compressors are commonly used on virtually every instrument in popular music recording. This includes snare and kick drum as well as guitar, bass guitar, piano, and vocals.

Noise gates are also level controlling devices and, because they serve essentially the reverse function of compressors, they are also called expanders. A noise gate allows the loudest signals (those above the threshold) to pass through unaffected, while lower level signals are attenuated. This effectively increases the dynamic range of the signal by making the quieter passages quieter, or even silent, relative to those sounds loud enough to be above the threshold (opening the "gate" and passing through unaffected). The primary purpose of the noise gate is to get rid of unwanted sound. For example, there may be extraneous sounds on a vocal take, such as shuffling of feet, clearing the throat, humming a note for pitch before singing, and so on. With a noise gate these extraneous sounds can be "gated out" (that is, set below the threshold of the gate so that they are attenuated) as long as they don't occur during the singing.

Noise gates have provided engineers with a great aid in cleaning up recorded sound, and this has been especially helpful in the recording of a live drum set. Because drums consist of so many instruments that are placed so close together, it is very difficult to achieve separation between the components. Without separation you may not be able to process each sound individually. For example, in the multitrack technique it is common to record the snare drum on a separate track. This means that you may process the snare drum separately from the other drums. But because the tom-toms and hi-hat are so close to the snare drum their sound will leak into the snare drum mic and be heard on that particular track. Then when you process the snare drum the same processing will be applied to the tom-tom and hi-hat sounds that have leaked onto the snare drum track. This may cause undesirable effects, such as reverb on the hi-hat. Noise gates allow you to isolate the various drums and cymbals from each other. You may run the snare track through a noise gate and set the threshold so that the snare drum sounds are loud enough to get through the gate, while the hi-hat and tom-toms are below the threshold and can be attenuated to virtual silence. Thanks to the use of noise gates, there has been a great improvement in the clarity of drum recording over the last ten years.

The delay effect has really been a part of the recording process since its inception, because delay is a natural by-product of sound reproduction in any environment. Sound waves invariably take many routes to the ear (or the microphone), and all except the most direct routes produce a delayed version of the sound. The effect is most obvious in a concert hall, but it occurs in any environment, and thus delays are commonly picked up by the microphone in the recording process. We call the delayed part of the sound the ambience of the environment. In early recordings the only control over ambience was the relative distance of the microphone from the sound source: the farther away from the source, the greater the ambience relative to the direct sound. Microphone placement is still a critical factor in recording.

In the 1950s the tape delay and the echo chamber began to be used, representing the two basic kinds of added ambience employed in recording today: delay and reverb. Tape delay is created by feeding the sound into a three-head tape recorder, recording the sound (on the second head) and playing it back milliseconds later on the playback head. (The first head is an erase head.) The delay sound reproduced on the playback head, the length of which depends on the distance from the record to the playback head, is combined with the direct signal to create an ambient effect. This kind of "straight delay" (an exact but delayed duplicate of the original sound) does not actually exist in nature, but it is close enough to a natural kind of ambience to be useful in creating spacial effects in recording.

An echo chamber is simply a small room, usually about the size of a walk-in closet. The sound being recorded is broadcast into the chamber through a speaker, and the very ambient reproduction is picked up by a microphone. This ambience or echo (now generally referred to as reverb, or reverberation) is then mixed with the direct signal. The engineer can control the amount of reverb that is added.

Both tape delay and echo chambers are still in use, though they are less common due to the current availability of digital devices that create these same effects, but with less noise and more precision. Digital delay creates discrete delay effects like those made with tape delay; digital reverb creates room ambiences of many delays, like the sounds produced in an echo chamber. With digital delay we can generate a greater variety of effects than with tape delay, especially given the flexibility it provides in setting up delays of different lengths.

Longer delay effects (generally called echo or "slapback") can be used to simulate very large environments. This is because the sound in a large space must travel to the far walls and then return, creating a long delay before the ambient sound is heard. Long delays may include what is usually called feedback, which recreates the effect of a sound returning from a far wall in a large environment, bouncing back to and from the far wall, causing a repeated delay. We simulate this by feeding the delayed signal, created by the digital or tape delay, back into the machine so that it goes through the delay process again, providing equally timed repeats. The more feedback, the greater the number of repeats. Feedback is used in short delay modes as well (as it can occur in small environments as well as large), though the effect is much less pronounced. An interesting side effect is that these long and repeated delays may create whole new rhythms of their own. By timing them in relation to the tempo of the music, one can set up these delays to interact with the music just as if they were a played part of the vocal or instrumental performance (though perhaps impossibly so). These types of repeated delay effects are becoming very common in popular music.

Reverb is a much more accurate, and thereby much more complex, reproduction of the kind of ambient sounds that actually occur in nature. Reverb is made of a multitude of delays and clusters of delays, much as in actual room ambience. Reverb has evolved from the echo chambers described above, through devices using springs and plates, to the current proliferation of digital reverb units. Digital reverb provides far more control over the parameters of the effect than any of the previous devices. Many different room environments and characteristics may be simulated with just one digital unit. While reverb does not provide the rhythmic possibilities of digital delay, it does have a powerful effect on one's perception of the overall sound, and thus of rhythm.

Reverb may be used to simulate a variety of natural environments, though it is also used to produce unnatural effects. Gated reverb, in which natural sounding reverb is gated so that only the first portion of the effect is used, has become a popular way of using large amounts of reverb without the clutter of the ambient decay washing over the background. Non-linear reverberation characteristics which are not found in nature have become popular. These effects do not have the linear decay that is natural to reverb, and they produce a booming sound that, for example, might effectively lengthen the sound of a snare drum. Reverb is what places a sound in an environment, and with digital reverb some pretty strange and unworldly environments have been created for music. In general, the combination of delay and reverb has provided composers, producers, and engineers with the ability to create a sense of space in a recording.

Mixing. A part of the process of multitrack recording is the job of mixing the numerous recorded tracks into a final two-track (stereo) version of the music. Along with various sound adjustments and signal processing (EQ, gating, reverb, and so on, some of which are applied at the time of recording and further developed during mixing), the mixing process involves setting instrument volume levels and choosing their positions in the stereo image.

Setting the levels of drum set components is a very subjective process, as is placing the entire drum set relative to the rest of the music. Generally speaking, the most prominent musical element should be the melody, with rhythm playing the primary support role and harmony (rhythm guitar and keyboards) in a secondary support role. In popular music this means that the snare drum and kick drum are generally mixed quite prominently, just below the level of the vocal or melody instrument. The hi-hat and cymbals are usually placed at a lower level in the mix, though the hi-hat may be emphasized in some circumstances. Tom-toms, when used as fills, are also brought out in the mix, as they draw attention to movement from one section of the music to another.

Stereo imaging refers to the placement of musical sounds in a continuum that extends from one speaker to another. Creative stereo imaging—assigning each instrument its own place in the continuum—can enhance recordings significantly, adding depth, movement, and the feeling of a spacial spread between the components of a band or orchestra. You position each recorded channel in the stereo image with the use of pan pots, which are usually rotary knobs located just above the master fader of each channel of the mixing console. The placement can be either hard left or right, center or mono (equal volume in both speakers), or various degrees of soft left or right. In soft left or soft right placement, the sound is louder in one speaker than the other, but is coming from both speakers to some degree. The feeling of a spacial spread can also be enhanced with the use of reverb and delay.

The use of stereo imaging in the recording and mixing of drums and drum machines can make a big difference in their effectiveness. The idea here is to recreate the spacial spread of live drums. That is, the stereo effect heard by a listener seated directly in front of a live drum set is translated to tape in both live drum and drum machine recordings. Using a standard drum set configuration, the image may be described as follows:

> Kick drum: center
> Snare drum: center
> Hi-hat: soft right
> Hi-tom: soft right
> Mid-tom: center
> Floor-tom: soft left
> Crash cymbal: soft right
> Ride cymbal: soft left

When adding other percussion sounds to the basic drum set, further imaging will be necessary to create a pleasing spread of sounds and to maintain distinction between instruments. Similar sounds, such as the closed hi-hat and shaker, can be separated by panning them to opposite speakers, e.g., hi-hat: soft right; shaker: soft left. The use of stereo imaging in recording drum machines will generally help to provide a realistic drum sound.

The mixing job also involves the application of sound processing and reverb or delay effects, the use of which will vary depending on the subjective ear. Some kind of reverb is generally applied to the kick drum, the snare drum, and the tom-toms. Occasionally reverb may be added to the hi-hat or cymbals, though generally these are left "dry" (without reverb). As discussed previously, natural and natural-sounding reverb may come from a variety of sources, and unnatural reverb effects have become increasingly popular on drums. Straight delay may also be used on any of the drums, and more radical processing such as chorusing or flanging can be applied to create special effects. Often you'll find that once you hear your processed instrument in the context of other musical parts, you'll feel the need to change the sound: the EQ settings may have to be altered, for example, or the reverb boosted. Experimentation is the key to the effective adjustment of drum sounds. In an overall sense, mixing is a delicate process of balancing level, tone, panning, and ambience.

Past, Present, Future. The application of computers, MIDI, and digitally-based sound modules has added new dimension to the basic multitrack recording process. Sequencers, as we've seen, allow you to program very complex, computer-controlled, MIDI-driven functions that trigger sound modules as well as much of the current processing gear. Through the use of time code, you may synchronize these functions with multitrack tape recorders. MIDI controllable delays and reverbs have already become common and very sophisticated. They may be programmed to respond to the same performance data that a sequencer uses to drive a sound module. Thus the delay time might be programmed to increase when notes are played with more velocity, or a reverb program may switch when it receives a program change message at any number of points during a timed sequence. Processing applications can be composed into a piece of music right along with the performance data.

These technologies are providing other new ways of working with music recordings. Advances in triggering techniques allow you to trigger sounds directly from tape and translate them into MIDI signals. Thus, live recordings of kick and snare drums are commonly replaced by electronic or digital drum sounds from any number of sound modules. The live drum from tape is simply used to trigger (via a MIDI channel message) the sound from the sound module. Most all the elements of a human performance, including variations in volume and in time, are translated into a completely different sound.

Various means of playing with the inconsistencies of human performance are probably the most exciting rhythmic developments in contemporary music. The ability to digitally translate, analyze, and manipulate timing and dynamic factors in rhythm performances opens up vast new areas of music production. However, these factors have been analyzed and manipulated by musicians for centuries with great subtlety and vision, if with much less sophisticated tools.

This marriage of recording and sound processing techniques with musical performance information, all expressed as digital data via MIDI, sets the mind reeling with its creative potential. It also leaves the mind a bit stunned with the load of technical information necessary to function in the current musical environment. Fortunately, you needn't know every twist and turn of the digital landscape, just as you needn't know every musical style or concept. A balanced base of knowledge for today's musician, however, includes drum beats, MIDI, sequencers, and basic recording technology, as well as music fundamentals such as notation.

The recording process is constantly changing as both the technology and the people who use it grow and develop. Stripped to its fundamental, however, music recording may be traced back from multitrack systems to the beginning of sound reproduction, to the system of notation, to the aural tradition, to speech itself, and finally to the basics of communication. Rhythm, as we have already found, is as natural to human beings as speech. Music is a fundamental means of human communication. The recording process is simply an extension of this most primitive of man's capabilities. And though technology will undoubtedly continue to undergo transformation, the essence of human expression through music will never change. The future is revealing a seemingly incredible world of computer-based wizardry, yet the technology itself is benign, and is capable of reflecting the human spirit only insofar as the creation of music is a mirror of that spirit.

BIBLIOGRAPHY

Apel, Willi, editor. *The Harvard Dictionary of Music*. Cambridge, Massachusetts: Harvard University Press, 1972.

Apel, Willi and Ralph T. Daniel, editors. *The Harvard Brief Dictionary of Music*. New York: Washington Square Press, 1968.

Carr, Ian, Digby Fairweather, and Brian Priestley. *Jazz: The Essential Companion*. London: Grafton Books, 1987.

Cooper, Grosvenor and Leonard B. Meyer. *The Rhythmic Structure of Music*. Chicago: University of Chicago Press, 1960.

Crigger, David. *How to Make Your Drum Machine Sound Like a Drummer*. Newbury Park, California: Alexander Publishing, 1987.

Feather, Leonard. *The Encyclopedia of Jazz*. Second edition. New York: Bonanza Books, 1960.

Gabriel, Clive and Rosamund Shuter-Dyson. *The Psychology of Musical Ability*. New York: Methuen and Company, 1982.

Harrison, F. L. and J. A. Westrup. *The New College Encyclopedia of Music*. New York: W. W. Norton and Company, 1981.

Jones, LeRoi. *Blues People*. New York: William Morrow and Company, 1963.

Landeck, Beatrice. *Echoes of Africa in Folk Songs of the Americas*. New York: David McKay and Company.

Mills, Elizabeth and Sister Therese Murphy, editors. *The Suzuki Concept: An Introduction to a Successful Music Education Method for Early Music Education*. Berkeley, California: Diablo Press, 1973.

Nketia, J. H. Kwabena. *The Music of Africa*. New York: W. W. Norton and Company, 1974.

Pareles, Jon and Patty Romanowski, editors. *The Rolling Stone Encyclopedia of Rock and Roll*. New York: Summit Books, 1983.

Rae, John. *Latin Guide for Drummers*. Los Angeles: Try Publishing Company, 1969.

Schuller, Gunther. *Early Jazz: Its Roots and Musical Development*. New York: Oxford University Press, 1986.

Stewart, Michael. "The Feel Factor." *Electronic Musician*, October, 1987.

Whitcomb, Ian. *After the Ball: Pop Music from Rag to Rock*. New York: Simon and Schuster, 1973.

INDEX

PHOTO CREDITS

ABOUT THE AUTHOR

Steve Savage is an independent producer/engineer, the author of several drum
    instruction books, and executive director of Blue Bear School of American
    Music. After fifteen years as a professional drummer, he currently divides
    his time between Savage Studios—a state-of-the-art 24-track studio in San
    Francisco—and Savage Thoroughbred Farms in Santa Rosa, operated by
    his wife Darlene.

Senior Editor: Tad Lathrop
Book and Cover Design: Bob Fillie
Music Typesetting: Don Giller